"One of the greatest contemporary Catholic ,   ,
an intellectual concerned with politics and attentive to
the unique reality of persons and things, humble before
what is objective and thus opened to the truth. One great
theme dominates De Corte's work the subjects of which
are only apparently divergent: the vigorous denunciation
of modern rationalism and an invitation to man to renew
a bond with reality, without which he cannot live as a
man. De Corte is above all a moralist and a philosopher
of the state of crisis. As he himself declared, two subjects
haunted him as a philosopher, the crisis of society and the
crisis of the Church."

— **DANILO CASTELLANO**, Italian philosopher and
author whose works include *L'aristotelismo cristiano di
Marcel de Corte*

"One of the greatest twentieth-century masters of the coun-
terrevolution." De Corte waged a battle of the intellect
"against the current 'dis-society' of modern democracy, total-
itarianism of the state, and the consumer society, and, at
the same time, for the restoration of man in the fullness
of his relationship to God, the world around us, and our
neighbors. A brave, tireless warrior."

— **JUAN VALLET DE GOYTISOLO**, Spanish jurist
and philosopher, author, among other works, of *Ideología,
praxis y mito de la tecnocracia*

"For centuries, since the moral insights of Plato and Aristotle, the virtues were considered as the heart of morality.
To be good meant cultivating virtue, a training of intellect
and will toward goodness which affected even the body.
Morality was not conceived merely as a dry adherence
to external rules but as a change of life, a true internal
transformation. It is this which Marcel De Corte, with so

many lively and interesting comments on contemporary society, brings to life in this series of books. They are an important contribution to what is known today as 'virtue ethics,' a cultivation of the soul as old nearly as philosophy but just as important for our moral life today."

—**THOMAS STORCK**, author, editor and translator, most recently author of *Economics: An Alternative Introduction* (XIII Books)

"The image of De Corte, obtained from his writings in *Itinéraires*, has remained with me, with his devastating analysis of: the epistemological reversal of modernity; the derangement of what is the product of this, the 'homo rationalis'; the irredeemable crisis of civilization; the corrupting character of politics founded on the 'religion of democracy,' and the tragedy which was — and still is — the crisis of the post-conciliar Church. De Corte, of an unsurpassed intellectual mettle, professed philosophical realism which is in perfect accord with his anti-modernism. The denial of an uncreated order of values leads to modernism and ends by negating tradition, religion and morality."

—**MIGUEL AYUSO**, Professor of Political Science at the Comillas Pontifical University, Madrid, and author of books on social and political topics, most recently, of *¿El pueblo contra el Estado?*

PRUDENCE

Prudence

MARCEL DE CORTE

Translated by Inez Fitzgerald Storck

AROUCA
PRESS

Taken from the 2nd edition published in
2019 by Dominique Martin Morin (Poitiers,
France). This English edition also includes
copious footnotes by the translator.

ISBN: 978-1-998492-19-0

Arouca Press
PO Box 55003
Bridgeport PO
Waterloo, ON N2J 3G0
Canada
www.aroucapress.com
Send inquiries to info@aroucapress.com

Cover illustration from a print
of the Four Virtues by
Hendrick Goltzius (1558–1617)

CONTENTS

TRANSLATOR'S
INTRODUCTION

EFENDER OF THE TRUTH as embodied in Aristotle and St. Thomas Aquinas; crusader denouncing deformations of the person and society, starting with his critique of Descartes; predictor of the collapse of civilization; and member of the Belgian resistance against the Nazis, perhaps Marcel De Corte could best be characterized as a militant prophet engaged in the intellectual, spiritual, and political battles of his times.

Born into a family of peasants in Genappe, Belgium in 1905, De Corte completed his secondary school studies at the Athénée Royal de Nivelles where he obtained the classical education offered by the school for four centuries. In 1928 he was awarded a doctorate in philosophy and classical philology from the Free University of Brussels, devoting his dissertation to Aristotle's concept of the intellect. He then taught classical languages at a secondary school for two years. With a scholarship from the Belgian government, De Corte resumed his studies at two prestigious institutions in Paris, the École normal supérieure and the Institut Catholique. Afterwards he conducted research on the work of Aristotle at four universities in Italy.

De Corte began his university teaching career at
the University of Liège in 1930, where he was named
a professor in 1940, holding a chair in the history of
ancient philosophy. The minister of education had
attempted to block this appointment, since De Corte
was known to be a Catholic. However King Léopold
III personally intervened in his favor. De Corte taught
at the university until his retirement in 1975. He died
in Belgium in 1994.

De Corte's first publications focused on specific
areas of philosophy: *La doctrine de l'intelligence
chez Aristote* (1934), *Aristote et Plotin* (1935), and *La
philosophie de Gabriel Marcel* (1938). Another text,
Descartes, philosophe de modernité, of uncertain date,
appeared posthumously in 2022. Then World War II
intervened, and the Nazi occupation of Belgium. De
Corte took an active role in the resistance, heading an
underground group operating in the Ardennes Forest.

After the war, De Corte began to engage in social
criticism, analyzing how society has been affected by
alienation, consumerism, increasing mechanization,
and a loss of the sense of the spiritual. He used the
term "dis-society" to characterize the resulting degradation of communal life. *Essai sur la fin d'une
civilisation* (1949, *On the Death of a Civilization*,
Arouca Press, 2023) was one of the first of these works,
followed by *L'homme contre lui-même* (1962) and
L'intelligence en péril de mort (1969, *Intelligence in
Danger of Death*, Arouca Press, 2023). On a personal
note, he and his wife Marie wrote *Deviens ce que
tu es: Léon, notre fils* (1956), the moving account of

their sensitive and precociously intelligent son, who had hoped to become a priest, valiant in his effort to overcome the effects of polio, but succumbed to influenza at age 18.

In addition to around twenty books, De Corte published hundreds of articles on moral philosophy, the philosophy of art, metaphysics, mysticism, economic philosophy and ancient and modern philosophers. Many of his articles appeared in the Belgian daily *La Libre Belgique* and *Itinéraires* (1956–1996), a traditional Catholic review published under the editorship of Jean Madiran and covering social and political issues such as the war in Algeria, education, socialism, and communism, topics related to the spiritual life and the changes resulting from Vatican II, toward which many contributors had a critical stance, including De Corte.

De Corte's books on each of the cardinal virtues, published from 1973 to 1982 — first published in the pages of *Itinéraires* — continue his social criticism. Far from treating the moral life of the individual in isolation from society, he situates each virtue in its social context, in its relationship to the political order and the economy. The deleterious effects on the social order when these virtues are neglected contribute to the degradation of society, threatening the survival of our civilization. As one of the major French-speaking Thomists of the twentieth century, along with Maritain and Gilson, De Corte follows the Angelic Doctor in his analyses, with numerous references also to modern philosophers and novelists, poets, and playwrights. Though he paints a dark picture of the current "dis-society," he does not leave us without hope for the future, for a renascent society and civilization rising from the ashes of today's decadent social order.

—Inez Fitzgerald Storck

I
THE TRUE MEANING
OF PRUDENCE

OR ARISTOTLE AND ST. Thomas, prudence is the most important characteristic in a man. It is what makes him a man in the full sense of the term. Through prudence he rules himself, directs his actions, orders himself to his final end as personal as it is specific, marshals in a single action all the elements of his being, and becomes an integrated and fulfilled person. The prudent man is the ideal man. "Maître[1] Robert," said St. Louis to his friend Sorbon,[2] "I would very much like to be well-known as a wise and prudent man, and would that I were such a man. As for the rest, I leave it to you. For a prudent man is something so great that just to pronounce these words gives delight to the tongue."

---

[1] A multivalent title in French, one of whose uses at the time was to designate the head of a school. [Tr.] —Footnotes not indicated as the translator's are De Corte's.
[2] The priest Robert de Sorbon (1201–1274) in addition to serving as confessor to King St. Louis founded a school, of which he was the chancellor, which was to become the University of Paris, the Sorbonne. [Tr.]

Charity itself is prudence. Even in the supernatural order, prudence has the first place, except when perfect charity has become the only guide of the soul. For if the three theological virtues give prudence the supernatural end that sets it in motion, it nonetheless regulates their action. Even though God may inspire supernatural acts of love, they are acts of man, rational and deliberate actions. "Believe me, my daughters," writes St. Teresa of Ávila to the nuns entrusted to her, "everything which separates you from reason separates you from God." This without a doubt refers to reason penetrated by divine light, and prudence elevated by grace. Yet grace does not destroy nature.

Contrary to all the enthusiasts, to all the enlightened who have unleashed openness to the world in the Church that they are destroying, and the opposite of the frenetic love of God of those who proclaim that every love is of God, the true practice of Christianity consists in the right *balance* as determined by prudence. The rule of the prudential golden mean actually has nothing to do with the ends of the supernatural life. As Father Gardeil[3] notes that with regard to the latter, "the law of excess reigns: *tantum potes, tantum aude, quia major omni laude*"[4] The measure for loving God will always be to love God without measure. We rightly call Him God, and not one or

[3] Ambroise Gardeil, OP (1859–1931), a Thomist important in the formation of many Dominicans around the turn of the century. [Tr.]
[4] As much as you can, dare that much, for He is greater than all praise. From the sequence for Corpus Christi written by St. Thomas Aquinas. [Tr.]

another of the current substitutions for Him. The law of the prudential happy medium concerns practical means, by definition always human, which man develops to attain the *goal* of charity: "to become fellow citizens of the saints and members of the household of God" [Eph. 2:19]. These means are *measured*.

They are not left to our imagination, less still to our supposed "creativity," and much less to the influence of political ideologies and utopias that today replace faith, hope, and charity or which dare to ascribe their own ends to these virtues. Our will, free in its choice of means, can ultimately opt only for those which reason, the faculty for discerning what is real and true, declares to be appropriate for our supernatural end. Reason can only do this by sorting through them, putting them in order, and imposing on our judgment, on our will itself, the right balance that objectively adapts them to their instrumental role in our supernatural destiny. It is prudence that establishes this correct middle way, rejecting excessive measures and eliminating those that are weak. Here as elsewhere *in medio stat virtus*[5]; virtue does not hesitate: it positions itself in the right middle way, which prudence reveals to it.

It is pointless to say that this supernatural prudence, based on reason, steadfastness, decisiveness, self-control and, in short, the refusal of any manner of subjectivism, no longer has a place in the Church. Infused prudence has suffered the fate of acquired prudence. The latter is not only out of usage, it has

---

[5] Virtue lies in the middle, that is, in moderation. [Tr.]

been removed from the language. Philosophers today
do not even know the word for it. We can pinpoint
the period when the phenomenon of prudence and
the word itself disappeared, in advance of so many
other treasures. It was in the eighteenth century. La
Bruyère still associates the idea of prudence with
the notion of human perfection: "In a wicked man,
there is nothing to fashion a great man: praise his
views and his plans, admire how he conducts himself,
exaggerate his skill at making use of the most apt and
quick ways to achieve his ends; if the ends are bad,
prudence plays no part in them; *and where prudence
is lacking, find greatness if you can.*"[6] Voltaire does
not hesitate, seventy-five years later, to call prudence
a "foolish virtue."[7] Kant pronounces its death sen-
tence, banishing it from the moral code. According
to him, the prescriptions for prudence are strictly
hypothetical since they are dependent on a supreme
good, the existence of which cannot be demonstrated
scientifically: if you want to enjoy the vision of God
one day, act according to the guidelines of prudence
and order the means you use to this end! How could
these means have an absolute, universal moral value?
With the way to transcendence blocked, there remains
only that of immanence. Beginning with Kant, all
morality, instead of depending on prudence, will
rely on conscience. It is from within the conscience,

[6] Jean de La Bruyère (1645–1696), French philosopher and moralist. The citation is from *Les Caractères*, 1688. Emphasis added
by De Corte. [Tr.]
[7] Letter to Jean-François de La Harpe, 1775. [Tr.]

separated from everything external to it, that moral values will emerge. The objectivity of prudence has gradually been replaced by the subjectivity of the individual conscience — the origin of the moral chaos where contemporary humanity is floundering.[8]

Moral theology had already preceded philosophy in its effort to take sovereignty away from prudence and give it to conscience. In the seventeenth century, under the influence of St. Alphonsus Ligouri, casuistry initiated the movement which, little by little, would set up the conscience, by definition always pertaining to the individual, as sole judge of good and evil.[9] Conscience was transformed into a kind of double of the human being, invested with the mandate to direct his acts, when in reality it only conducts a quick internal review of the intelligence or imagination[10] or both at the same time. This review could not be extended without breaking off the

[8] Kant postulated a subjective principle, the categorical imperative, for evaluating the morality of human actions, according to which individuals should act according to guidelines that they deem applicable to everyone. See his *Groundwork for the Metaphysics of Morality*, 1785. [Tr.]

[9] In combating the legalism and Jansenism of his day, St. Alphonsus (1696–1787) discussed the significance of the subjective factor in sin, which could diminish, but also intensify, the degree of guilt. While emphasizing the importance of a properly formed conscience, he articulated principles to guide the conscience in doubtful matters. Later theologians distorted this teaching to the point of circumventing authoritative moral principles. St. Alphonsus was named Doctor of Moral Theology by the Church. See his *Moral Theology*, 1748. [Tr.]

[10] Here "imagination," following the usage of Aquinas, refers to mental images of existing things, not illusory things conjured up by the mind. [Tr.]

relationship of the faculties of the intellect, the will, and the passions with the external world, placing the subject, thus mutilated, into permanent schizophrenia.

The *hypostasierung*[11] of conscience, raising it up as a separate mental reality, the seat of the moral law, of the meaning of obligation and duty, as well as the source of remorse for having transgressed against them, is a myth which does not stand up to scrutiny. It is a dangerous myth that continually orients morality towards subjectivism. The innumerable examples of the *Tractatus de Conscientia*[12] that turned the minds of clerics (and lay people) in on themselves and on their mental representations have contributed much to substitute ratiocination for reality, utopia for existence, and a conception of the world as malleable material onto which — through the force of their will — they imprint their disincarnate ideas. St. Thomas was quite careful not to grant to conscience an exaggerated place in the moral actions of man. The significance that he gave to objectivity anticipated the degree to which continual self-reflexivity — an unhealthy tendency in so many intellectuals disconnected from reality — undermines morality and ends up making the supernatural natural. This is what we are witnessing today: the disappearance of the virtue of prudence has engendered the emergence of a substitute, which in turn has degenerated into a vice. One cannot designate otherwise the "collective

[11] German, hypostatization, treating a concept as a distinct reality. [Tr.]
[12] Treatise on conscience. [Tr.]

conscience," an alibi for all the abdications and refus-
als of responsibility. This is a point of confluence for
individual "consciences" debilitated by autophagic [13]
withdrawal into themselves and manipulated by the
stage managers of this world who make use of them
as a battering ram to overthrow the last vestiges of
the moral order.

Is it then astonishing to note that the word *prudence*, formerly so rich in positive connotation, has
only a negative meaning, and as the latest dictionaries
maintain indicates the "mental attitude of someone
who, reflecting on the impact and consequences of
his acts, takes steps to avoid mistakes and possible
problems and refrains from everything he believes
could be a possible source of harm." It is enough to
calculate the distance separating the prudent man
of St. Louis and the "prudence" of Monsieur Joseph
Prudhomme, the character created by Henri Monnier
in 1857, who afflicted him with the mediocre, smug
character of one full of himself and lacking any ability
to express what is real other than through sententious,
inane banalities. [14] The prudent man has become one
who does not face up to the *reality* of his existence
and his *objective* destiny. He deals astutely with others,
with the expectation that they in turn will deal with
his pitiful self the same way. He takes *precautions*

[13] Referring to the body's process of eliminating old and damaged
cell parts to promote survival. [Tr.]
[14] French playwright and caricaturist (1799–1877). See his play
Grandeur et décadence de Monsieur Joseph Prudhomme (1857);
prudhomme means "prudent man" in French. [Tr.]

with regard to future events *out of fear* that they
could impinge on his fragile person, crushing him.
His motto is "avoid trouble," and the monster of
history swallows him up.

Yet "words are the only thing worth fighting for,"
as Chesterton assures us.[15] If current parlance only
accepts the word *prudence* in its debased meaning,
the ability to dodge the pitfalls and risks that are
part of human life, if the prudent man now only
appears in the technical meaning of the *Conseils de
Prud'hommes*[16] composed of those in the workplace
who are given the responsibility to judge disputes
between employers and employees in the same trade
or profession, if prudence is in a state of hibernation
in most people today, this is no reason to let it die
of hunger and cold as it becomes permanently numb.
Furthermore, the resurrection of the Church, guardian of morality and sacrament of salvation for men,
is tied to the resurrection of prudence.

We must fight for the true meaning of this word in
order to save the reality that it signifies. Along with
prudence, the fate of man is at stake. The Greek *kalo-
skagathos*,[17] the Latin *civis romanus*,[18] the Spanish
hidalgo,[19] the *honnête homme*[20] of the seventeenth

---

[15] *The Ball and the Cross* (1909). [Tr.]
[16] As explained in the text, tribunals of "prudent men" in France
which settle disputes between employers and employees over
work contracts. [Tr.]
[17] In ancient Greece, gentlemanly personal conduct. [Tr.]
[18] Roman citizen. [Tr.]
[19] A member of the nobility without a hereditary title. [Tr.]
[20] French, gentleman. [Tr.]

century, and the English gentleman[21] are no more. But if the prudent man embodied in them has died along with them, if prudence does not subsist in the depths of the soul, ready to be reborn when it is called forth, humanity has come to the end of its course. An irreversible *mutation*, as the foolish put it, will transform *homo sapiens* into *homo faber*[22] and as we shall see at the end of our study, this man is an entity who has not been given a name in any language and who has become the slave of technology, of which he is the sorcerer's apprentice.

[21] In English in the text. [Tr.]
[22] Man the maker. [Tr.]

II

THE PATH TO HAPPINESS
AND WISDOM

OR ST. THOMAS, PRUDENCE
is "the most necessary virtue for the life of
man."[1] It is a good counselor in matters
relating to man's entire life and the ultimate
end of human life.[2] It is "the art of right
conduct."[3] "There can be no moral virtue without
it."[4] Operating in each virtue, it is at work in all of
them *sicut sol aliqualiter influit in omnia corpora*,[5]
that is, just as the sun sheds its light on all bodies.
Similar to a charioteer, who with his two feet firmly
set on the floorboard of the chariot, guides it to the
finish line of the race, prudence directs all the virtues
to their realization.[6] Its main role is to govern the life

---

[1] *Summa Theologiae* (afterwards *ST*) I-II, q 57, art. 5, c.
[2] *ST*, I-II, q. 57, art. 4, ad. 3; art. 5, ad. 1.
[3] *ST*, I-II, q. 58, art. 2, ad. 1.
[4] *ST*, I-II, q. 58, art. 4, c.
[5] *ST*, II-II, q. 47, art. 5, ad. 2.
[6] It is the *motor* [Latin, driving force] and the *aurigo virtutum* [charioteer of the virtues] according to *ST* III, Suppl., q. 2, art. 4, c, which adds: *ideo quaelibet cum motu proprio virtus moralis habet aliquid de motu prudentiae* [Consequently, each moral virtue in addition to its proper activity has something of the activity of prudence. (Tr.)]

of man.[7] In a compact formula, cited a thousand times, the unfathomable depth of which we need to comprehend, it is the *recta ratio agibilium*, that is, right reason applied to practice.

Since this is the case, it is important in the first place to recall what *human actions* are for St. Thomas.

Every act is defined by the end to which it is directed. This end is always a good. Even if an act is directed to something evil, that evil is still held to be a good by the author of the act. The good and the end are thus identical. This is a fact immediately grasped by the intellect. Yet as there are a multitude of actions, there will be a multitude of ends and goods. Experience shows that these ends and goods have among themselves relationships of subordination and hierarchy: a person pursues one specific end in view of another, which in turn functions as a springboard for a third object desired, and so on, up to the end point, that constitutes the final goal of man. All the ends connected to each other are thus in the last analysis linked to an end that is not willed in view of another, which on the contrary is willed for itself, commonly called *happiness* or *beatitude*. "All men want to be happy, even those who are going to be hanged," writes Pascal,[8] echoing the wisdom of the ages expressed by Cicero: *Beatos nos omnes esse volumus.*[9]

[7] *ST,* II-II, q. 47, art. 13, c.
[8] Free citation from *Pensées* (1670). [Tr.]
[9] We all want to be happy, *Tusculan Disputations*, c. 45 BC. [Tr.]

What then is that happiness without which human action is unintelligible, if not something in a state of completion, a state where nothing is lacking to man and his fulfillment, having nothing to do with what in him is accidental,[10] transitory, incidental, or extrinsic, but concerning what is essential, permanent, universal, intrinsically proper to him, that is, to his own manner of functioning: that which distinguishes him from all other living beings, reason. The human act is thus a rational act. However, since reason can be considered either in its proper activity, which is to know, or inasmuch as it directs the irrational part of man, it has two kinds of operations: what we call intellectual operations and moral operations. The intellectual virtues, understanding, knowledge, artistry or craftsmanship, and wisdom[11] are perfections of man's ability to reason. The moral virtues, justice, fortitude, and temperance, and the retinue of virtues revolving around them, come into being when reason penetrates the irrational part of man. Where then can we find happiness?

"One understands by happiness," writes St. Thomas, "nothing other than the perfect good of an intellectual nature, which is capable of knowing that it has a sufficiency of the good which it possesses."[12] Happiness is thus defined by an act and by the object of this act. It consists in a lasting, perfect satisfaction,

[10] In the philosophical sense. [Tr.]
[11] See Aristotle's *Nicomachean Ethics*, VI for a discussion of the intellectual virtues. [Tr.]
[12] *ST*, I, q. 26, art. 1, c.

involving a relationship with the object which produces the satisfaction. Happiness thus has two aspects,
inseparable from each other, the objective: the reality
the possession of which obtains happiness; and the
subjective: the delight felt by the agent in the act of
possessing this reality. The reality that makes us completely happy is *objective beatitude*; all the acts through
which we enjoy it, and the enjoyment itself, constitute
subjective beatitude. The reality is the *cause* of the
happiness; the delight is its *essence*; the operation or
set of operations which obtains happiness for us is the
means of attaining to that reality which will be for us
our supreme good. Obviously subjective beatitude is
subordinated to objective beatitude, *sicut finis sub fine*,
that is, as an end subordinated to another end. [13] It
follows from this that subjective beatitude, the only
one which we are able to experience, is necessarily an
imperfect participation in objective perfect beatitude.

Experience is sufficiently illustrative of this, since
"if happiness is the perfect, sufficient good, it excludes
every evil and fulfills every desire. But in this life
every evil cannot be excluded, since the present life
is subjected to many unavoidable evils: ignorance, on
the part of the intellect; inordinate affection, on the
part of the appetite; and many afflictions, on the part
of the body... Similarly, we are unable, in this life,
to satiate the desire for the good. For man naturally
wants the good which he possesses to be abiding.
Now the goods of the present life are fleeting, since

[13] *Commentary on Sentences* [hereafter *Sentences*] II, D. 38, q.
1, art. 2.

life itself passes away, this life which we naturally desire, which we would want to possess abidingly, for man naturally shrinks from death. It follows that it is impossible to have true happiness in this life."[14]

Moreover, "it is impossible for the happiness of man to lie in any created good. For happiness is the perfect good which completely satisfies the appetite; it would not be the final end if there remained something else to be desired. Now the object of the will, that is, man's appetite, is the universal good, as the object of the intellect is universal truth. Hence it is evident that nothing can satisfy man's will except the universal good. This is to be found, not in any creature, but in God alone, because every creature has goodness by participation. Thus God alone can satisfy the will of man ... Therefore God alone constitutes man's happiness."[15] On the other hand, we are unable to love the perfections of the Supreme Being without knowing Him, without representing Him to ourselves *by means of concepts*, which we draw from the world experienced by the senses. It follows that our concepts are inadequate when applied to this immaterial, simple, infinite Being who is God. The love for Him that we profess will always then be imperfect, precarious, unstable, and inconstant. Grace itself, while it surpasses human nature, will only allow our love to attain to God through the darkness of supernatural faith. To possess God as He is in Himself and to participate everlastingly in

[14] *ST,* I-II, q. 5, art. 3, c.
[15] *ST,* I-II, q. 2, art. 8, c.

His intimate life, man must wait for the life to come
when God in His infinite generosity will be simultaneously the object (*id*) of his knowledge and love
and the means (*quo*) by which he attains to them.[16]

Yet man does not cease to pursue happiness in
his present life. The problem which arises is then
to know what kind of happiness *can be attained*
by man in the course of his earthly life. *Attainable*
happiness would be *real* happiness, the deficiencies
of which grace here below not only makes up for;
it also prepares relative perfection for its conversion
into absolute perfection, wholly accorded in the kingdom of God, which is not of this world. *Gratia non
tollit naturam*, that is, grace does not suppress nature.
The natural is the foundation of the supernatural.
It is the *bonum essentialissimum*,[17] the good most
conformed to human nature. Though grace is on
a higher level than nature, it is more important for
man to live according to nature than according to
grace: *Homini est essentialius esse naturae quam esse
gratiae, quamvis esse gratiae sit dignius.*[18] It is wrong
to preserve the gratuitous crowning of the human
being while taking away from him his foundation.
As Jorge Laporta writes, the gift of grace, far from
overthrowing, abolishing, or replacing the natural
order of things, complete in itself, *establishes* it. Grace
"does not suppress the natural in order to replace it

---

[16] *Summa contra Gentiles* III, 51.
[17] The most essential good. [Tr.]
[18] Nature belongs more to man's essence than grace, although
grace is more excellent. [Tr.] *ST* Supplement, q. 49, art. 3, c.

with an unexpected economy. On the contrary, the supernatural only crowns the work, and gives it perfect balance."[19] "For Thomas..., the natural desire to see God existing in every intelligent creature is above all an intellectual, voluntary act... As an intelligent being, [man] was made for this. He knows nothing about this, he denies it, he loses his time looking elsewhere for his happiness? Nevertheless, *naturaliter appetit visionem*,[20] that is, his being is constituted to behold the supreme Truth."[21] "But if this destiny is attainable, it is impossible for a created substance to achieve it through its own power...: an intelligent creature is defined by an end that it cannot attain through its own resources."[22] Such is the glorious secret of human nature: "a tremendous disproportion between what this being desires above all, irresistibly, often unconsciously," because he was born from God and his beginning is his end as well, "and that which this same creature can hope for and determine to win. A disparity, a mark of greatness!... The more grace appears to be gratuitous... the more nature itself stands out as great... For the incredible gift of God does nothing other than complete this humble creature...: *gratia est perfectio naturae*"[23]

[19] Jorge Laporta, *La destinée de la nature humaine selon saint Thomas d'Aquin*, Paris, 1965, p. 124.
[20] He naturally desires the vision [of God]. [Tr.]
[21] Laporta, p. 43.
[22] Ibid., p. 59. Cf. p. 61: "Every intellectual creature is defined by a destiny inaccessible to him through the power of his nature alone."; also pp. 95 and 100.
[23] Grace is the perfection of nature. [Tr.] Ibid., p. 127 and *Sentences* I, D. 3, q. 1, art. 1.

"For we are his offspring," Paul had proclaimed [Acts 17:28], after the Greek poet, in the Aeropagus at Athens.[24] The seal of God is permanent. But it is impossible for us to fill up the space within us, designed for the infinite, of our own power, since this space is placed within a finite, limited substance, incapable on its own of receiving an infinite substance. The most basic common sense cries out: to bridge the distance which separates the finite from the infinite, God's gratuitous gift is necessary. Sartre had an inkling of this, when, with one last grimace at the end of his tiresome inquiry on *Being and Nothingness*, he wrote that man is haunted by his desire to become God, "but this is a futile passion." [25]

Nothing could be more mistaken, not only on the level of grace, but also on the level of nature itself, where man in all his actions tends towards his absolute final end, which is God, just as a falling stone is drawn to the center of the earth. If happiness is a specifically human act,[26] it reaches its level of perfection in man in the act in which his intellect is most fully itself, that is, wisdom (*sophia*),[27] which encompasses all aspects of the contemplative activity of the soul, beginning with the comprehension

[24] The phrase begins, "as even some of your own poets have said"; some scholars hold that Paul was referring to the Cretan poet Epimedides, sixth century BC, an important figure in Athenian tradition. [Tr.]

[25] 1943. [Tr.]

[26] According to Thomas, happiness is an act; otherwise it would be pure potentiality. See *ST*, I-II, q. 3, art. 2, c. [Tr.]

[27] Thomas Aquinas, *Commentary on Aristotle's Nicomachean Ethics*, Marietti edition [henceforth *CNE*], 2134.

of the first principles of knowing (*intellectus*) in their radiant truth and the demonstration of the first causes of being and the ultimate principle of all reality (*scientia*), up to the ensemble of consequences which follow from the universal primacy of these principles.[28] The proper function of wisdom is to contemplate the order in the world and to comprehend the presence of God in all creatures, reflected in the mind as in a mirror. This is why wisdom is called *contemplative or speculative*.[29] The happiness it brings is sufficient unto itself and is sought for itself, "because it produces nothing outside of the act of contemplation, while all other activities of man bring us more or less significant advantages, distinguished from the activities themselves."[30] Far from being "useless," this "passion" allows man to ascend to the vision of the relation of the parts to the whole, of consequences to their cause, and of all things to their end, in which consists the harmony of the world.[31] This is the pinnacle of happiness: *videre dispositionem divinae providentiae est maxime delectabile*,[32] that is, to contemplate the order in the universe wrought by divine providence is exceedingly delightful. Nothing surpasses this joy born of the contemplation of

[28] Ibid., 1175, 1177, 1181, 1182, 1190, 2086, etc.
[29] *Sentences* III, D. 35, q. 1, art. 2.
[30] Aristotle, *Nicomachean Ethics* [henceforth *Nic. Eth.*] X, 7, 1177 b and *CNE* 2097.
[31] Ibid. Also *ST*, I, q, 42, art. 3, c: *ordo semper dicitur per comparationem ad aiquod principium* [Order always has reference to some principle. (Tr.)]; *ST*, I-II, q. 1, art. 4, c.; *De Veritate*, q. 5, art. 1, ad 9; *ST*, I, q. 21, art. 1, ad 3 and q. 47, art. 3, c.
[32] Aquinas, *Commentary on the Psalms*, 26 (27).

the truth, *gaudium de veritate,*[33] which continually
brings us back to God as its source.[34]

However, as Aristotle says, an exclusively contemplative life "is too lofty for the human condition,
since man insofar as he is a man does not live in
this way, but insofar as a divine element is present
in him."[35] The man who gives himself to contemplation does not live strictly speaking in a human
manner, but like higher substances whose nature is
purely intellectual. He stands in a kind of continuum
with angels[36] and, through grace, with God,[37] very
imperfectly, it is true, and in keeping with the weak
power imparted to his intelligence, *in homine autem
imperfecte et quasi participative.*[38] However, this weak
element is superior to all the rest: *et tamen istud
parvum est majus omnibus aliis quae in homine sunt.*[39]
Mary has chosen the better part and it will not be
taken from her [Luke 10:42]. The contemplative life,
absolutely speaking (*simpliciter*), is superior to the
active life. Nothing prevents one thing from being
in itself (*secundum se*) of a higher value than another
thing, while being, from a particular point of view
(*secundum quid*) surpassed by that other thing.[40] "If

[33] *ST,* I-II, q. 3, art. 4, c; cf. Aquinas, *Commentary on 1 Timothy,* 3,
L. 3.
[34] Aquinas, *Compendium of Theology,* 107.
[35] *Nic. Eth.* X, 7, 1177b; *CNE,* 2105–2110, pertinent to the text
which follows above.
[36] *Sentences* III, D. 35, q. 1, art. 2, quaestiuncula 2, ad 1.
[37] *ST,* I-II, q. 3, art. 5, c.
[38] But in man imperfectly and by participation. [Tr.] *CNE,* 2110.
[39] Ibid.
[40] *ST,* II-II, q. 182, art. 1, c.

it is true that the intellect is preeminently man himself"[41] and "if man, when he lives in accord with his intellect, assumes the kind of life most appropriate to him,"[42] "it obviously follows that he who gives himself to the contemplation of the truth is happy to the highest degree, as far as a man can be said to be happy in this life."[43]

St. Thomas, like Aristotle, considers that the contemplative life based on the activities of the intellect alone (the orientation of which is elevated by the theological virtues) is necessary for the happiness of man. One should not listen to the masses who, following the poet Simonides[44] urge mortal man to enjoy only perishable nourishment. "Man must (*debet*) tend toward immortality to the extent that he can, and, in keeping with what is in his power, live according to the intellect, the most noble of human faculties, its immortal and divine portion."[45] Yet since man is made of body and soul, and human nature is characterized by both the senses and the intellect, the life apportioned to him (*vita homini commensurata*) is seen to consist in the governing of the activities of the body and senses by his reason (*videtur consistere in hoc quod homo secundum rationem ordinet affectiones et operationes sensitivas et corporales*).[46] Such is the moral

[41] *Nic. Eth.* X, 7 in fine.
[42] *CNE*, 2109.
[43] *CNE*, 2110.
[44] Simonides of Ceos (c. 556–468 BC), Greek lyric poet. [Tr.]
[45] *CNE*, 2107.
[46] *CNE*, 2105.

life in the domain of the human: *circa humana*.[47]

Nec hoc est contra id quod supra dictum est: there is no contradiction between this affirmation and the primacy of the contemplative life[48]: "One goes from the active life to the contemplative life in the order of time (*secundum ordinem generationis*), but one returns from the contemplative life to the active life by way of direction (*per viam directionis*), that is, in order to submit the active life to the direction of the contemplative life."[49] The moral life governed by prudence has priority for us (*quoad nos*) over the contemplative life. However, because man is not only ordered to the fulfillment of his human nature, but also to the contemplation of the divine, it is a question of a temporal and temporary priority. In disciplining the passions of the soul and submitting them to the order of reason, the active life is a preparation for the contemplative life, always imperfect before ending in the life to come, but in and of itself of an excellence as perfect as is possible here below.[50] By nature, the higher use of reason, which is contemplation, has the same relationship to the lower use of reason in charge of action, as a husband has to his wife, who should be directed by him, according to the doctrine of St. Augustine in *On the Trinity*.[51] The active life that takes place in time, is then actuated and directed by

[47] *CNE*, 2106.
[48] *CNE*, 2110.
[49] *ST*, II-II, q. 182, art. 4, ad 2.
[50] *ST*, II-II, q. 182, art. 3, c
[51] *ST*, II-II, q. 182, art. 4, c.

the contemplative life towards an end which surpasses it — the fullness of the contemplation of God at the end of the present life.[52]

Between prudence, that governs the active life and directs all the moral virtues, and wisdom, which governs the contemplative life and all the intellectual virtues, the ties are as close as possible. Prudence considers what leads to happiness, and wisdom considers the object of happiness itself.[53] The particular greatness of a virtue is measured by its object. Wisdom, which considers the highest cause to be God, by which it judges subordinate causes, imposes its judgment on prudence, which concerns human matters. It would be otherwise if "man were the greatest of the things in the world"; such is not the case, as Aristotle himself states.[54] Thus wisdom must govern prudence, which must then prescribe for men how they ought to attain wisdom, even in its most practical form, prudence in politics. "Prudence leads to wisdom, preparing the way for her, like the doorkeeper of the king."[55] As a result, wisdom is a magnetic pole that attracts prudence, its radiance pervading prudence and drawing it near. Yet in accord with the fundamental principle according to that which is last in the order of execution is first in the order of intention, prudence itself is the principle of wisdom. Wisdom is the actuating force of prudence in two ways. The first relates to

[52] Ibid.
[53] *ST,* I-II, q. 66, art. 5, ad 2.
[54] *ST,* I-II, q. 66, art. 5, ad 1.
[55] Ibid.

the status of the creature that is man, who like every being which comes forth from the divine goodness, tends towards returning to it animated by a natural love of God. The second concerns the very nature of prudence, which to regulate the conduct of human life, requires from the start an adherence to a general principle, from which will follow particular and concrete acts. We recognize *synderesis*[56] here, the highest law of practical reasoning, a superior *habitus*,[57] "which contains the principles of the natural law, which are the first principles of human actions."[58]

Now the natural law is nothing other than the participation of the human creature in the eternal law that exists in God and governs all created things.[59] The first principles deriving from it, self-evident, are the counterpart in the practical order of the first principles in speculative reasoning. To the principle of identity[60] in the speculative order corresponds the principle of doing good and avoiding evil in the field of action, and also, adds St. Thomas, a certain general concept of life (*aliqua scientia practica*[61]) — a knowledge of the true ends of man and his destiny. St. Thomas did not analyze in detail the elements of this general concept of life, knowledge of which was

---

[56] Self-evident truths in the field of moral conduct. [Tr.]
[57] Meaning "habit"; the plural is also *habitus*.
[58] *ST,* I-II, q. 94, art. 1, ad 2.
[59] *ST,* I-II, q. 91, art. 2, c.
[60] According to which a thing is identical to itself; every object exists as something specific, and cannot exist as something else. [Tr.]
[61] Some practical knowledge. [Tr.]

in his time widespread in all minds, even the most uncultured, in varying degrees through the agency of the Church and the Catholic state. We will see below that these later resembled each other in accepting and respecting the common good and the laws that embodied it. Without the existence of a stable social order in which a lived wisdom is transmitted from generation to generation fully recognized and practiced by the ruling elites and reflected through them in the people, prudence disappears and gives way to substitutes that are disruptive of human conduct. *Causae ad invicem sunt causae*[62]: wisdom found throughout society governs prudence and prudence directs the moral virtues towards that very wisdom that prudence reinforces. Nothing is compartmentalized or sealed off in the spiritual order.

The active life of the human being composed of soul and body is then for all who possess a human nature or for most of them (*omnibus vel pluribus habentibus humanam naturam*) the seat of human happiness attainable here below.[63] It is facilitated by prudence and the moral virtues, of which prudence is the guide. *Virtutes compositi, proprie loquando, sunt humanae, inquantum homo est compositus ex anima et corpore, unde et vita quae est secundum has, id est secundum prudentiam et virtutem moralem, est humana, quae dicitur activa. Et per consequens felicitas, quae in hac vita consistit, est humana. Sed vita*

---

[62] Causes are mutually causes for each other, referring to the mutual interdependence of causes. [Tr.]
[63] *CNE*, 170.

et felicitas speculativa, quae est propria intellectus, est separata et divina.[64] Contemplation itself cannot be without these virtues, since it presupposes the moral virtues associated with prudence as a prior disposition (*dispositive*).[65] Prudence is, from this point of view, the human virtue par excellence. It is prudence that perfects human nature and directs it with firmness and ease toward what Maurras admirably calls "the summit of wisdom."[66]

[64] Now virtues of the composite being, properly speaking, are human inasmuch as man is composed of soul and body. Hence life in accord with these, namely, prudence and moral virtue, is also human and is called the active life. Consequently happiness consisting in this kind of life is human. But contemplative life and contemplative happiness, which are proper to the intellect, are separate and divine. [Tr.] *CNE*, 2115.

[65] *ST,* II-II, q. 180, art. 2, c.

[66] Charles Maurras (1868–1952), French journalist, politician, and poet, the principal exponent of the monarchist, anti-revolutionary movement, L'Action française.The quote is from his collection of poetry *La Balance intérieure* (1952). [Tr.]

III

THE CORRECT USE OF REASON IN MAKING CHOICES

THUS, PRUDENCE IS THE most noble of our *habitus*. We know that this *habitus* perfects all human activities by ultimately orienting them ever more decisively towards their final end. In making these activities function in a particular direction, according to their respective ends and operating on specific objects, it gives them a facility, promptitude, and ease in action, lacking to all those who neglect these *habitus* or abandon them according to their changing moods. Moreover, we take pleasure in continually carrying out specific virtuous acts. *Firmiter, expedite, delectabiliter*[1]: when these three indications are found in man's rational activities, we find ourselves in the presence of a *habitus*, of an abiding disposition to action which, far from being mechanical and monotonous, proves to be dynamic, adaptable, versatile, always ready to spring into action.[2] The

---

[1] Steadfastly, promptly, with delight. [Tr.]
[2] Aquinas, *Disputed Questions on Virtue* [hereafter *On Virtue*], q. 1, art. 1, c.

habitus, writes John of St. Thomas[3] in his baroque Latin, are *turgentia ubera animae*, that is, breasts filled with life, always ready for action when so prompted. Thanks to these *habitus*, man acquires that ease in acting that allows him to direct the disordered impulses of his faculties towards their respective objects, to impose a norm for behavior on them, to guide them to their proper end, and to govern himself. In this regard, it is enough to observe the man who possesses the *habitus* of justice, fortitude, and temperance to note that he is master of himself, holds the reins of his conduct firmly, and directs his actions easily and happily towards their end. Such *habitus* are *virtues*.

Now virtue implies not only self-control, an upright will, and control of the irascible and concupiscible passions, but also *the good use of them*. We are also masters of ourselves in vice, even if later vice becomes our master. This is why the purely intellectual virtues, understanding, knowledge, and even, in a certain sense, wisdom — *video meliora proboque, deteriora sequor*[4] — are not virtues in the full sense of the word. The art of making things, which is also a *habitus* of the intelligence, is even less of a virtue. We can use our knowledge and technical skills for evil. We can even cover wicked undertakings with a veil of wise or erudite words, look at Tartuffe![5]

---

[3] Portuguese Dominican theologian and philosophy professor (1589–1644). [Tr.]
[4] I see what is better and approve, but choose what is worse. Ovid, *Metamorphoses*, VII. [Tr.]
[5] 1664 play by Molière, in which the eponymous character Tartuffe feigns virtue to achieve evil ends. [Tr.]

Grammar gives us the ability to speak correctly. But it does not make us speak correctly, since we may be familiar with grammar and yet voluntarily commit a solecism or barbarity.[6] We cannot use virtue for ill; we cannot use prudence to do evil. "It is impossible to be prudent if one is not good."[7] Thus, as we shall see below, prudence, as "the virtue which takes counsel, makes judgments, and directs rightly (*recte*) in view of the good end of man's entire life,"[8] must be first oriented towards this good end, or it is nothing more than guile and astuteness. One can be learned and base at the same time. One cannot be truly a man without making good use of one's properly human activities. The intellectual virtues, the arts, and technical skills do not perfect man by informing him of how to use them well. This is why they are not virtues on an equal footing with prudence and the moral virtues.[9] For there to be virtue as it is defined, the *habitus* must not be purely intellectual, but also resulting from the use of the will. This is the case with prudence, the highest virtue of practical reason, seated in the intellect and thus intellectual due to its essence and its object, and moral due to its matter; justice, fortitude, and temperance, and virtues related to them are also moral virtues due to their matter.[10]

Prudence, then, plays a pivotal role in man: it brings together the intellect and the will in the virtue

[6] *ST,* I-II, q. 56, art. 3, c.
[7] *Nic. Eth.* VI, 12, 1144a.
[8] *ST,* II-II, q. 47, art. 13, c.
[9] *On Virtue,* q. 1, art. 7, c.
[10] *ST,* I-II, q. 58, art. 3, ad 1.

of justice.[11] The intellect, the will, and the passions in the virtues have to do with the irascible and the concupiscible appetites. Justice concerns man as both a rational and social animal, while the latter virtues involve elements constitutive of man in his entirety. Prudence is the most human of all the virtues since it goes back to the general principles of human acts in order to apply them most aptly to the particular, concrete, and contingent.

The famous Aristotelian definition of virtue, repeated by St. Thomas, enables us to have a good understanding of this: virtue is a *habitus*, a stable disposition of the will consisting of the choice of a mean, a golden mean determined by right reason with regard to our situation of and in accord with what a prudent man would decide on.[12] Let us recall that the first characteristic of a virtue is to be "a habitual state which directs and assures the correct execution of an action."[13] The second is to attain the mean that for the author of the act in question is the right one: in his circumstances and place in society if it is a matter of justice, with regard to the endurance he should display in the trials of life if it is a matter of fortitude, and concerning the influence of reason on the desires of the lower functions of his being if it is a matter of temperance. This just mean is always a middle point between two opposite extremes, too much or too little, an excess or a deficiency. The golden mean of justice

---

[11] Justice is a virtue of the will.
[12] *Nic. Eth*, II, 6, 1106b.
[13] *ST,* II-II, q. 182, art. 4, c.

is not the same for a superior as for a subordinate because their contribution to the common good is not identical; it is normal to require more of a king than of a mere citizen. The just mean of fortitude is not the same for a man, woman, or child, and it is different for an athlete and a weakling. The particular circumstances of an action are further modifying factors. In the presence of a range of them, mistakes are common and easy to make: all it takes is to cede to one pressing demand or another. It is much harder to act uprightly, because only one line of action matters, the right one, the one that hits the center of the target, the one determined by *right reasoning*.

Right reasoning is appropriate reasoning, proper to the particular situation in which one finds oneself. It is the reasoning that supplies the correct norm, and not a general rationale that would place the act, looking at it superficially along with all other similar acts, into a pre-established category. The right use of reason is like the *quick look* of the artisan who discerns from one or another indication of the material he is working on what he must do: add to or take away, wait or speed up. In short, what needs to be done in a particular case, what is adapted at that juncture to the end he is pursuing, what he must select, decide on, bring to a halt, or adjust as a function of his objective, towards which he is purposefully working. Here it is not enough to know general rules that apply to one or another undertaking, but the golden mean in a particular case. He who possesses only a general rule does not know enough to proceed further in the field of action, which is always specific. For example, if a person, responding to someone who asked what should be given to a person with a specific illness, replied to him "what medicine dictates" or "what a doctor gifted with the art of healing prescribes," he would not know what really should be given to the sick person based on the cause of the illness. To know this, it is necessary to have recourse to right reasoning, to right reasoning in the area of craftsmanship if it is a question of an object to make, to the right reasoning of prudence if it is a matter of an important human act.[14] It is thus necessary to adapt general norms for action to the case in point so that they become a relevant, appropriate, and sufficient guide. That is to say, the norm of the just mean for the act accomplished *hic et nunc*[15] in its particular concreteness. This is the task of prudential right reasoning.

For virtue to exist, there must be: first of all an inclination towards an end, an appetite or desire, and second, a choice determined by reason of the means adapted to this end, so that the means is not wanting due to excess or deficiency. The desire must be consistent not only with the end that is pursued, but as a function of the hierarchy of ends, with the ultimate end of human life. The determined norm for action, as it results from the use of reason, must obey the law that governs every act of reason: to conform to reality in order to be correct. It is clear that the uprightness of the appetite is a requirement for

[14] *CNE*, 1110–1111.
[15] Here and now. [Tr.]

right reasoning: if the desire is not suitably directed to the proper end of man, the reasoning can be all that you would wish, except correct. Conversely, if the appetite is well-ordered, but the reasoning used errs in its choice of the appropriate rule of conduct, the act will never attain its end. As Aristotle says in a formula that admirably summarizes this twofold, indivisible aspect of a moral act: "Both the reasoning must be true and the desire right, and the latter must strive for what the former affirms."[16] It follows that the choice, with the appetite and reason as principles, is the work of *reasoning impelled by a desire* inasmuch as it is in essence an act of the intellect; it is also the work of *a desire informed by the intellect* inasmuch as it is in essence an act of the appetite directed by reason.[17] Now as the object of the choice is in the final analysis a good or an evil thing, themselves objects of the will and not of the intellect (which is concerned with the true and the false), it would be better to state that the choice is an act of the will as guided by the intellect.[18] Therefore, truth in a practical matter will not involve, as it would in a theoretical matter, thought in accord with being, but rather reason in accord with the rectitude of the appetite. The right reasoning of prudence will then always be the use of reason that deliberates and chooses as a function of desire rightly directed towards the ultimate end of human life: the happiness of man, inasmuch as he

[16]   *Nic. Eth.* VI, 2, 1139a.
[17]   *CNE,* 1129.
[18]   Ibid., 1137

is composed of intellect and will, and soul and body.

Yet now it is a self-evident maxim that according to what a man is, so does his end or *raison d'être* appear to him.[19] All the lines of reasoning concerning human acts indeed proceed from material man, made of flesh and blood: *et tale principium est homo, scilicet agens.*[20] It is important, then, for the author of the act to be oriented *in reality*, and not just in his thinking, to the *true* Sovereign Good for correct prudential reasoning to make its choices effectively. In other words, man must first be good, since "vice perverts the judgment of reason and leads us into error about principles of conduct."[21] Only the man who is good can make a judgment about the Sovereign Good because he adheres to it in all his conduct. The practice of the moral virtues of justice, fortitude, and temperance and the related virtues must then precede the exercise of prudence. It is impossible to be prudent without being virtuous.

On the other hand, we know that it is impossible to be virtuous without being prudent, since the definition of virtue includes correct prudential reasoning. With diamond-like clarity, St. Thomas proves this to us: "Moral virtue can exist without certain intellectual virtues, for example without wisdom, knowledge, or art, but it cannot exist without understanding or prudence. Without prudence, there can be no moral virtue.

[19] *Nic. Eth.* III, 5, 1114a–b; *CNE*, 1273.
[20] *CNE*, 1137. [Man is a principle of this kind, namely, an agent. The rest of the phrase quoted: choosing by means of the intellect and appetitive faculty. (Tr.)]
[21] Ibid., 1274. The citation is from Aristotle.

Moral virtue is the habit of making good choices (*habitus electivus*). Now for a choice to be good, two things are necessary: first, that the intention be directed to a proper end, and this is the work of the moral virtue which inclines the appetitive power towards a good which is in harmony with reason, which is the end which should be pursued; second, that one use rightly the means which lead to the end, and this can only be done if his reason is able to counsel, judge, and command rightly, which is the work of prudence and virtues associated with it ... There is thus no moral virtue without prudence, nor, consequently, without understanding. It is through understanding that we know self-evident principles in both speculative and practical matters. Thus just as right reasoning in speculative matters presupposes an understanding of naturally known principles inasmuch as it proceeds from those principles, so too with prudence, which is right reasoning about conduct in life."[22]

There is no vicious circle here. The fact that the moral virtues precede prudence is at once ontological and psychological. It comes from the undeniable primacy exercised by the end over the means and from the fact, also indisputable, that the *habitus* of justice, fortitude, and temperance are first acquired under the influence of the social milieu and the example given by the elite. It is only subsequently that prudence appears, in the degree to which man, endowed with practical reason, exercises self-dominion in ever broadened areas of his life. As long as man has not acquired

[22] *ST*, II-II, q. 58, art. 4, c.

the ability to govern himself, he is not for that less virtuous, since his virtue is not dictated by prudence, but by correct opinion propagated within the society of which he is a member.[23] The moral virtues are the fruit of education received within the various groups we belong to, first and foremost, the state. This is not only the case with youth, but also for those who have reached the age of maturity: in fact, most people obey the demands and prohibitions of laws rather than following a line of reasoning, motivated by the fear of punishment rather than a sense of the good.[24] Prudence thus develops as a function of the increase of the moral virtues in those who, drawn to the common good of the state as a *desideratum* and to the universal common good which is God, are able to govern themselves and others who are not so privileged, and to provide correct prudential reasoning for them.[25]

Prudence reaches its highest, overarching point in the ruler who personifies the ideal of the prudent man par excellence.[26]

This is why St. Thomas, following Aristotle, attributes one last characteristic to virtue: it consists in the choice of the golden mean, a mean adapted to the correct end that is pursued. A mean we determine by the right use of reason, one that a prudent man would choose.

---

[23] Aristotle, *Politics*, III, 4, 1277b; *ST*, II-II, q. 47, art. 2, ad 1.
[24] *Nic. Eth.*, X, 10, 1180a; *CNE*, 2150.
[25] *Nic. Eth.*, VI, 8, 1141b; *CNE*, 1197.
[26] *ST*, II-II, q. 47, art. 12, c. in fine.

I V
CONFORMITY TO REALITY

E SEE TO WHAT point Aristotelian and Thomistic morality relating to prudence is conformed to the reality of human acts and their end. There is nothing less subjective then these moral principles, nothing that refers less to the "demands of individual conscience," still less to the "demands of the conscience of mankind." Nothing more adapted to the fluid, transient, concrete contingencies of acts that the moral virtues direct towards their end, and of which prudence is the rule.

At first glance, the axiom that is the basis for this morality, "according to what a man is, so will the end for which he is striving appear to him," could seem to be the clearest expression of subjectivism. The good could then vary with the particular state of mind of each individual, as influenced by his fanciful imaginings. This is not at all the case. The goodness, or malice, of the end does not depend on the idiosyncrasies of a person. Just the opposite is true. Aristotle, in fact, understands here that the end or Sovereign Good is

only evident to the eyes of the good man.[1] The man
formed through the discipline of the cardinal virtues
has been given an understanding of the fundamental
good of the final end he pursues. Such a man will
consequently judge all other ends in light of his virtu-
ousness because he himself is conformed to the "One
Thing Necessary" with every fiber of his reason and
will. This is the happiness he cannot dispense with,
whatever he may do, and that which he perceives to
be true *reality*. The virtuous man is then attuned to
the impulse that directs him *firmiter, expedite, delectabiliter* towards the true end of his existence. All
the particular, contingent acts that he performs *in
this sense*, which would otherwise be deprived of any
meaning, take on an understandable depth revealing
his luminous destiny to him. Consequently, he possesses the key that opens to him the mystery of his
being and, more precisely, becomes part of him as he
habitually and unfailingly follows the path it indicates to him. From this point on all his behavior has
a meaning, not because he gives it one, nor because
in his radical autonomy he creates his own law, but
because his conduct has in his own eyes and those of
an observer, a *real object* that he is striving for and
attains. What could be more realistic, more objective,
than this morality that points out to us the ontological
and psychological structure of the human act?

The only presupposition this morality allows, sanc-
tioned by the universal wisdom of the ages, is that it is
better to be virtuous than malicious, just than unjust,

[1] *Nic. Eth.*, VI, 12, 1144a.

strong than spineless, and temperate than glutton-
ous, drunk, or licentious. Moreover, common sense
approves this when it observes that vice inevitably
blocks all forms of intelligence, even the astuteness it
seems to hone and which in the end is always made
less penetrating by passion. The conduct of the man
of vice is disordered, chaotic, ultimately sinister, and
as his reasoning grows dull, reduces him to what is
a state of pure imagination, an exonerating myth, a
makeshift ideal, an emptiness devoid of reality, or
quite simply, the absence of thought of an animal.

The same objectivity characterizes the golden mean
for the person concerned, which prudence is dedicated
to finding, and that the imprudence of the majority
of contemporary Thomists call the *subjective mean*.
St. Thomas carefully avoids this designation. It is not
a matter here of a mean determined by the subject
through an arbitrary decree of the inventive will, freed
from adhering to norms of behavior, convinced that
it is able to generate its own rules. It is impossible to
escape from the imperative of the final end; if we are
reasonable, we must try to organize all our actions
around this reference point, which will never lead us
astray. We can no longer avoid this dilemma: either we
turn to the *practice* of virtue in order to truly understand it, or we give up on this, and cunningly fabricate
a fallacious system of self-justifying morality in order
to put our faculty of reason in line with our disordered conduct. The truth in moral matters is defined as
rightly-directed desire corresponding with reason. This
proper orientation is only seen in virtuous behavior.

As a man is, so is the end that he pursues. This truth of practical reasoning is not less objective, nor less certain or less reliable than truth derived from speculative reasoning. It is supported on as solid a bedrock, but, once again, the mere practice of virtue brings this to light. If we are unsure about this, then we have not fostered the virtuous *habitus* or enabled it to develop within us. If we reject it, it is due to an initial act of liberty, most often completely forgotten, by which we have declined to lay the foundation for the *habitus* of virtue, and on the contrary have opted to build on the sand of superficial appearances and its continual erosion.

The golden mean of prudence is established on an objective foundation, which, we cannot say too often, does not come from speculative reasoning, but from practical reasoning operating according to the virtuous *habitus* and incarnated in the course of a transient moral act, which, along with many past acts, will help to confirm the right way that leads to the final end of human life. Prudential reasoning, grounded in this reality, is provided with a criterion that allows it to make objective judgments without self-indulgence. It can thus find the norm of the golden mean appropriate to the subject and the circumstances of the act he is carrying out. This norm, bringing together the concrete reality of the act and its proper orientation, will be suitable for the subject considered as an object. The ethics of Aristotle and of St. Thomas have nothing of "situation ethics," which is inadmissible, the fantasy of all manner of existentialists with their subjectivity: their narcissistic behavior is all too evident.

The prudential choice of the means suited to the end of the virtuous act not only participates in the objectivity of this end, but is one and the same with it. If there is only one way to hit the center of the target (and innumerable ways of missing the mark) — aiming the arrow in the right direction — the means lead directly to the end and becomes one with it at the very moment of attaining it, like a quivering arrow at the center of the its target. Therefore it is futile to see a contradiction in the *Summa Theologiae* between question 47, article 6 in II-II and question 66, article 3, ad 3 in I-II. The first assures us that "it does not pertain to prudence to provide the moral virtues with their end, but only to regulate the means." The second affirms that "prudence directs the moral virtues not only in choosing the means to the end, but also in designating the end." In the concrete act, carried out *hic et nunc*, the means is only distinguished from the end logically, and, conversely, the end is already present in the selection of means, in accord with the saying *ultimum in executione, primum in intentione*, that is, that which is last in the order of execution is first in the order of intention. The means is already present in the end at the very moment it is directed to the end, reversing the order in the same adage, *primum in intentione, ultimum in executione*. It is moreover all too clear, as Cajetan[2] underscores, that prudence has something to say about the end pursued, working towards it

[2] The Dominican theologian Thomas Cajetan (1469–1534) wrote a commentary on the *Summa Theologiae.*

and ordering all things so as to attain it. Moral virtue, then, executes the order received from prudence which allows it, through the use of suitable means, effectively to reach the correct end within its purview.

Prudence has the function of ordering, in both meanings of the word simultaneously: commanding and putting in order as it determines the means chosen for the end that is pursued. This shows its superiority over all the moral virtues. These, being *habitus*, only give the soul a subjective inclination to attain their proper end, while prudence, consonant with their rectitude and selecting the means suitable for the attainment of their end, enables them to reach it and to bring it into existence. By means of prudence, the end becomes really and existentially objective: it brings the end from potency to act. Now, "a cause is always superior to its effect . . . Hence, the cause and root of human good is reason," with the good defined as the adaptation to necessary reality or to contingent reality[3], as is the case here. "Prudence which perfects reason surpasses in goodness the other moral virtues which perfect the appetitive power inasmuch as it participates in reason."[4] The preeminent nobility of prudence among all the human virtues derives from its intellectual nature, through which and in which is manifested the objectivity of practical reasoning, the faculty concerned with what is realizable. The archer who aims his arrow at the center of the target

---

[3] This appears to refer to God (the necessary reality) and created things (contingent reality). [Tr.]

[4] *ST*, I-II, q. 66, art. 1, c; *On Virtue*, q. 5, art. 3.

knows that he is directing it to this goal, while the goal, though it is the object desired, is unaware of it. Prudence is given the reason for its existence from the moral virtues, but enables them to understand their acts. Once more, we see that prudence is the most human of the virtues, the virtue of the intellect, and as such superior to the virtues of the will.

It is also the most human of the virtues in that it is the virtue of the intellect that works in essential collaboration with the senses in order to accomplish and order the moral act in its specific, contingent reality. It is totally oriented to reality here: it embraces both the universal and particular, the necessary and the accidental. Though the practical certainty of prudence is not at the level of speculative certainty, it compensates by bringing into play all the faculties of the human being.

Thus we have seen that the *recta ratio* of prudence, an intellectual virtue, is based on its conformity to a well-ordered appetitive faculty that only exists in the virtuous man, the best example of what it is to be human, so that the *conformitas ad appetitum rectum*[5] is not at all subjective. Moreover, the upright intention of the moral virtues is enlightened by prudence, which brings the act to fruition through the selection of the appropriate means. Every choice comes from deliberation and reasoning. All reasoning begins with principles and ends in a conclusion. We have before us here a "practical syllogism" in which the major premise is established on the *truly* human ends that the virtuous

---

[5] Conformity to a right appetite. [Tr.]

man strives for, ends which in turn are perforce derived from the first principles of conduct, particularly from the very first: one *must* do good and avoid evil.

This is not a moral obligation from which one can exempt oneself by a free act; it is the sine qua non of acts: *man can only pursue the good; he can only avoid evil.* This good derives its actual content from the practice of the virtues. The absence of these virtues or the presence of vice changes or destroys in man what makes him a man: the intellect and will. The moral virtues practiced by a good man receive their ultimate end or their principles — since the end is the principle of all actions — from the natural law. These principles, immediately comprehended by reason, constitute, as we know, *synderesis.* Practical knowledge, like speculative knowledge, begins with principles that are naturally known. According to St. Thomas, the common principles that prudence relies on in its deliberations *are more connatural to man*, or as Aristotle remarks, because life according to speculative reason is beyond what is natural to man.[6] "Synderesis hence moves prudence, in the same way that the understanding of principles moves science."[7] Synderesis is the equivalent in practical matters of the understanding of principles in the speculative domain. It is the foundation of the deliberations or counsels of prudence, as well as the determination of the appropriate means. These steps in the operation of prudence are parallel to those governing speculative

[6] *ST*, II-II, q. 47, art. 15, c; *Nic. Eth*, X, 7, 1177b.
[7] *ST*, II-II, q. 47, art. 6, ad 3.

research. In both areas their governing principles serve as the necessary foundation.

St. Thomas makes a clear comparison: "Prudence is right reasoning applied to acts to be carried out. Hence the main act of prudence must be the main act of reason with regard to what can be done. There are three such acts. The first is to take counsel, which is connected to inquiry," since deliberation involves looking into matters. "The second act is *the judgment* about what one has discovered. *And speculative reasoning goes no further here.*"[8] "But practical reasoning, directed to action, goes further, and its third act is to command," bringing the act to fruition through what has been counseled and decided on. "And since this act is closer to the end of practical reasoning, it is the principle act of practical reason and thus of prudence."[9] "This third act is proper to the practical intellect, inasmuch as it is ordered to action." Indeed, speculative reasoning does not command; it contemplates, observes, and draws conclusions. But for acts that we have to carry out, it is obvious that a command from practical reason is necessary. "To govern pertains to the order of action; it is the principle act to which all other acts are subordinated," and depends on "this virtue, prudence, which has to do with commanding well."[10]

---

[8] This refers to the order of the necessary sequence of steps: one goes from the general to the specific through a closely connected series of judgments in the practical as well as the speculative order. Emphasis is De Corte's.

[9] *ST*, II-II, q. 47, art. 8, c.

[10] *ST*, I-II, q. 57, art. 6, c.

In its first two stages, prudence resembles speculative reasoning with regard to what is logically necessary. However, these two stages are only the preparation for the essential: the insertion of the act into
life, carrying it out in reality. One who deliberates
well, deliberates so as to attain the end, and it is the
same with one who judges well.[11] And the end is
the *specific, concrete, contingent* act that depends only
on prudence and the will which complies with its
orders. For "to move, absolutely speaking, pertains
to the will, while to command implies movement
accompanied by a certain ordering" that guides it.
Thus, it is an act of prudential reasoning.[12] Prudence
is concerned with the universal and the particular.
It considers not only universal principles of acting,
though a universal principle is not capable of moving to action, prudence also has to be cognizant of
the particular, as it is the principle of all action and
every action is particular. This is why those who do
not have knowledge of universals carry out certain
acts better than others who have this knowledge:
their superiority comes from their experience in a
particular area. For example, if a doctor knows that
light meats are easily digestible and advantageous to
health, but does not know which meats are light, he
cannot help the sick person get well. Since prudence
provides the reason for an action, the prudent man
must have knowledge of both the universal and the
particular. If one had to choose, it is better to have a

[11] *Nic. Eth.*, VI, 9, 1142b.
[12] *ST,* II-II, q. 47, art. 8, ad 3.

knowledge of particulars, which are more proximate to the act.

Prudential reasoning, which ends in a specific, contingent action, involves knowledge of the universal principles of synderesis and the general concept, more or less developed, of man and the world discussed above, but it equally assumes knowledge of the particular act which it must accomplish or not accomplish. Prudential reasoning thus corresponds fully to the definition of man as a "rational animal." Reason is the faculty in which universals are seated and the senses are the faculty that enable us to grasp the individual act in its singularity. The observation of animal life shows us what this practical ability to sense is: it corresponds to the realm of action of the external senses, from which the speculative intellect abstracts what is intelligible. Whence comes the flight of the lamb from the wolf before the experience of the threat which it constitutes, all the while following a dog obviously resembling the wolf? Whence comes the fact that the ewe gives her milk to her lamb while refusing it to another? Why does the sparrow make its nest with wisps of straw and not twigs, which are more or less similar? The external senses do not recognize perceptible objects as useful or harmful, good or bad. Nor does the imagination,[13] which processes sense data. Therefore, there must be in the animal the ability to discern the efficacious from the ineffective, the beneficial from the harmful,

---

[13] Here, where impressions received from the senses are stored and mental images created. [Tr.]

what is good with regard to the end pursued (obtaining food, building its nest, perpetuating the species) from what would be detrimental to it. The ancients called this faculty the *estimative* because it "estimates" the utility or harmfulness of an object. Man, as an animal, is provided with the estimative faculty, but since his practical reason is always in touch with it, like his speculative reason with the external senses, it is referred to as *cogitative*, which conveys the idea of discursive operations and deliberation.

There obviously must be a cognitive faculty that presents an object as beneficial or dangerous, but which is intimately united to the appetite. In fact, while other animals through their natural instinct receive specific representations of reality in connection to the accomplishment of a particular action of pursuit or flight, man arrives at them through a kind of inference, or *collatio*,[14] which synthesizes individual representations, as reason synthesizes universal representations. This is why the cognitive faculty is also called the particular reason, or *ratio particularis*.[15] The act of reasoning is the result of the union of the faculty of sensing with the intellect.

It is an act of the intellect concerning a perceptible object and understanding the particular entity as it is. *Hunc hominem prout hic homo, hoc lignum prout hoc*

[14] *ST*, I, q. 78, art. 4. c; *CNE*, 1123.
[15] Idem. [Aquinas uses the term *ratio particularis* to refer to practical reason as applied to specific situations. See the *Commentary on Aristotle's De Anima*, III, lect. 16, no. 845, in which he also refers to a universal particular reason, which determines which fundamental moral principle should be applied. (Tr.)]

lignum, that is, this man here taken as just this man, not another, and as such man, and this piece of wood taken as this piece of wood, not another, and as such wood. In the practical domain, the act of the intellect concerns this specific action that must be carried out, not another one, in view of the end prescribed by the corresponding moral virtue; this then applies to human acts in general. The human act comprehends the individual *ut existens sub natura communi*,[16] through a reflexive intellectual operation in the sense that he goes back to previous specific acts, which he recalls and associates in what is suitably called the experience of life.[17] The intellect apprehends them, replete as they are with what is universally human, as it brings the heights of synderesis down to their relationship to concrete life. The intellect is able to know reality as apprehended through the senses better than the senses can perceive it.[18] It comprehends, along with the uniqueness of the present reality, the universal that this reality implicitly bears within it. The intellect makes distinctions among specific mental representations, compares them, sorts through them, and finally selects one which through its creative power will inspire a new representation relating to a given case. Prudence will command the will to incarnate this representation into existence in conformity with the virtue it relies on to reach its end.

---

[16] As existing with (literally "under") a common nature. [Tr.]
[17] Aquinas, *Commentary on Aristotle's Metaphysics*, I, lesson 1, nos. 15 and 16.
[18] *ST*, I, q. 78, art. 4, ad 4.

Cogitative or particular reason is thus the faculty that brings together moral acts from the past, evaluates them with respect to the end it has in mind, and determines how the content of the acts accords with synderesis. From there it derives a universal law adapted to the given case or rather notes in the specific case, the universal law concerning the good to pursue and evil to avoid. This is exactly what Maurras, in his admirable expression, calls *organizing empiricism*: by going back to and scrutinizing past moral acts and their deep connection to the true destiny of men, the particular reason establishes the proper tool or criterion that the prudent man will actually adapt to the virtuous act he brings to execution.

But it is clear that only the prudent man can suitably determine this criterion, which the particular reason formulates. Aristotle and St. Thomas explicitly affirm this in their definition of virtue. Most people do not have the intelligence to join the universal and the particular in one cognitive act. They obey a prudential tendency common in the social milieu where they find themselves, a product of the moral elite, which, so to speak, serves as guardian over their weak intellects. It is an axiom, confirmed by facts to be the most striking of truths, that man is the most imitative of animals. He will unfailingly imitate those in charge of the society he belongs to. To behave as he pleases is just unthinkable. Anti-conformity soon comes to be widespread and becomes the worst of conformities: the normalization of what is aberrant.

Thus, if it is true that it is better in practice to have a knack, a certain turn of thought, an adroitness, prudence in the most concrete sense of the word, as we have said above, then it is better yet to have this aptitude and also to recognize what elicits it and how it works. In fact, "men of experience know that a thing is so, but they do not know why. Those skilled at crafting things" (and the prudent man in the lofty sense of the word) "know the causes of the things that are made" (as well as how they are made). This is why we think that the heads of every enterprise deserve greater consideration than the workers: they are more knowledgeable and wise since they know the causes of everything that is made (and the techniques used to make them), while the workers are like inanimate objects who act, but without knowing what they are doing, in the manner that fire burns. But while inanimate objects carry out each of their functions by virtue of their nature, the workers perform them through habit. [19] This habit comes from virtues that the leaders have inculcated in those under them and which make up the way of life — and the moral level — of the society they belong to. *Humanum paucis vivit genus*, that is, the human species lives thanks to very few men. [20] Such a law does not admit of any exceptions,

[19] Aristotle's *Metaphysics*, I, 981a and 982b; Aquinas, *Commentary on Aristotle's Metaphysics*, I, lesson 1, 24–28. Aristotle's text is on the speculative level. We have added parenthetical remarks to bring it to the practical level.

[20] From the *Pharsalia*, a long epic poem by the first-century Roman poet Lucan. The verse has also been translated in a more pessimistic sense: The human species lives for the sake of a few. [Tr.]

neither on earth nor in heaven. It provides the most
solid foundation possible for collective prudence: the
social and political. Let us not, however, anticipate a
conclusion that a study of the texts imposes on us:
ideal prudence is political, and if prudence is indeed
the most human of virtues, politics, *humanly speaking*, is the noblest task of man in his life here below.
Maurras was incontestably right to state: *Politics first*.

As we can see, cogitative or particular reason is
the soul of prudence, the virtue of the golden mean:
not only does its truth conform to the nature of
mankind, but also to any individual endowed with
human nature and engaged in action in an individual
capacity; action is always concrete and specific. When
as a function of its accumulated experience prudential
reasoning chooses the norm appropriate for a given
case, it does so because the norm corresponds to the
reality of similar past acts: it is true, in that it conforms to this reality. When it is aligned to the good
end it pursues, it is also conformed to a truly human
end, *per conformitatem ad appetitum rectum*.[21] Nothing is more objective, we never tire of repeating, than
prudential reason. It is always commensurate with
reality. As for the truth of practical intellectual virtue,
or prudence, if one relates it to things, it shows itself
to be measured to them. In this regard, the mean is
taken to be conformity to reality in the practical intellectual virtues as in the speculative. But in relation
to the appetite, it has the character of a rule and a

---

[21] In conformity with a right appetite. [Tr.]

measure.[22] In other words, prudence is the measure of the appetite because *it is itself first measured* by the morally good end that it strives for and then by both the universal and particular reality to which it is conformed in the particular reasoning which it employs. Prudence is an intellectual virtue, of which things themselves are the measure and rule.[23]

In any case, as we observe, it is not a question of "conscience" for a single minute. It is always a matter of adapting one's faculties, intellectual or affective, to reality. Now "conscience is not a faculty, but an act."[24] Conscience is always concerned with the relationship between knowledge and some matter. When one says that conscience attests, obliges, prompts, or, again, accuses, blames, or corrects, this comes from the actual application of our knowledge to our action. Its rule is always subjective. In effect, the decision I make with my conscience does not at all affect the rest of men. If a cannibal feels himself obliged in conscience to eat human flesh, which is what his own conscience dictates to him, it imposes no obligation on the consciences of others. It follows that the rule of conscience is purely individual. It does not rely on any universal principle as prudence does, but only on itself. The norm of conscience is essentially fallible, and the proof is that there is a correct conscience and an erroneous conscience. The first is in no way correct in itself since there is

22 *ST*, I-II, q. 64, art. 3, c.
23 *ST*, I-II, q. 64, art. 3, ad 2.
24 *ST*, I, q. 79, art. 13, c.

always the possibility of error: its correctness does not come from its essence, but presupposes the *recta ratio agibilium*, which is prudence, and its twofold objective truth: the universal and the particular. Furthermore, a correct conscience obliges not because it is correct, but inasmuch as it is the conscience, since an erroneous conscience obliges.

This is why beyond the fallible rule of conscience, we need an infallible rule: this is given to us by prudence. Correct prudential reasoning is correct, or else it would not exist. *Corrupta ratio non est ratio.*[25] It is an abuse of language to speak of false reasoning: false reasoning is not reasoning. "The man who reasons badly does not reason, he talks nonsense."[26] Thus, one understands why St. Thomas does not insert conscience into his theory of morality as moderns mistakenly do. The subjectivity and fallibility inherent in conscience are radically opposed to the objectivity and practical infallibility of prudence, always characterized by correct reasoning, good judgment, and good governance; otherwise it does not exist. It is not conscience that establishes morality, but rather prudence alone with its fully human realism.

This realism shines forth in the constituent elements of prudence. We will consider only two of them here, memory and docility.[27]

[25] Corrupt reason is not reason. [Tr.] *Sentences*, II, dist. 24, q. 3, art. 3, ad 3.
[26] In French, "L'homme qui raisonne mal, ne raisonne pas, il déraisonne." [Tr.] Father L. Lehu, *Revue thomiste*, 30, 1925.
[27] For the integral components of prudence, see *ST*, II-II, q. 49 in its entirety.

Let us recall that prudence has as its object contingent human acts. With these, the directives it imposes cannot always be correct, as what is contingent could materialize or not. The truth with regard to the contingent does not always and everywhere appear as it would in the realm of the necessary, though it does most of the time and in the majority of cases. Now what is true most of the time and in the majority of cases can only be known through experience. One knows, for example, that thus and such a medication which has cured Tom, Dick, and Harry will cure nearly all the sick people afflicted with that illness. Experience is always the product of a great number of recollections stored in the memory. Nothing, though, is more realistic than memory: it can undoubtedly be mistaken, but one will never remember what has never been. The veracious character of the memory comes from its fundamental relationship to events which have really occurred, with events just as they happened. Similarly the knowledge of history, which is essentially a function of memory, is a factor in prudence, the director of upright human conduct: history, *magistra vitae*, that is, the mistress of life, provides prudence with countless examples of choices made by people and their consequences, advantageous or deleterious, inscribed in events. It is in referring to these acts, which are enlightening for prudence, to what has already been accomplished, which consequently has an undeniable compelling force, that prudence deliberates, chooses, and commands. It knows through memory and past experience that taking a certain stance has been fruitful, or, on the contrary, detrimental. The exigency of the past is for prudence a light projected onto the contingent aspects of the act that it directs. It is only from the past that it derives its foresight and grasp of the future which, by definition, has not yet come into being and so cannot, as such, be the object of true knowledge. Without the past, the only period of time that does not change, which definitively exists and thus escapes from contingency without the *real, objective* presence of the past in the heart of the memory, prudence could not possibly provide the correct reasoning for actions to be carried out. In imbibing the reality of the past, prudence gives weight to the choice of the means that will lead to the end envisioned to reality and the truth. The past gives it an understanding of the future, breaking through the darkness in which it is enshrouded.

Thus the rupture with the past that we have been witnessing for two centuries is the worst enemy of prudence, replacing it with an ideology that takes the place of self-governance and, through a clever dose of disembodied abstractions and unrestrained passions, drives human actions — if one can still characterize them as such. The political mythology of the "new man" and the "new society" insinuates itself in the space vacated by the disappearance of prudence, dead from lack of nourishment. Imaginings about the future liquidate the reality of the past. "People are led blindly by the imagination," wrote Napoleon, familiar with the subject. Uprooted from the past, man is completely incapable of governing himself. He is manipulated by powerful wills foreign to his destiny. The verse from the *Internationale*, "Let's make a clean slate of the past," inaugurates the puppet show, where the marionettes are sometimes in a state of panic, sometimes as disciplined as robots. This is contemporary "society," where those who pull the strings and the ventriloquists of public opinion know how to manipulate the controls.

There is no perfect prudence, suited to the reality of the means and the end, without *docility*. As we have said above, prudence has to do with specific actions to be accomplished. In this order of things, there is infinite variety, and it is not at all possible for a man not to have a gap in his knowledge of everything bearing on the matter; he only learns about this over time and not in one brief instant. This is why prudence is an area where man has an unusual need for the insights of others. The aged, above all, are qualified to enlighten him, those who have come to a sound understanding of the ends in practical matters (*qui sanum intellectum adepti sunt circa fines operabilium*). Whence these words from the philosopher in Book VI of the *Ethics*[28]: "It is important to attend to the sayings and opinions of old people and prudent men and to believe in them no less than in demonstrations, since due to their experience they perceive principles," *propter experientiam enim vident principia*. It is said in the

---

[28] *Nic. Eth.*, 1143b.

book of Proverbs [3:5], with the same meaning, "Do not trust your own prudence" and in Ecclesiasticus [6:35], "Stand in the midst of the ancients that are prudent, and unite yourself with your heart to their wisdom." This is why docility is rightly held to be part of prudence. Study and practice effectively work together to perfect a natural capacity for docility, in the sense that man, carefully, diligently, and respectfully, applies his mind to the teachings of elders, not neglecting them out of laziness or scorning them out of pride. Docility disposes one to accept the correct opinion (*rectam opinionem*) of another, and engenders astuteness (*eustochia*),[29] which enables one to arrive at a correct evaluation by oneself, in an easy, prompt conjecture about what is best to do in the matter at hand.[30]

It is hardly necessary to dwell on the virtue of docility, an integral part of prudence. In our age of delirious individualism, both docility and prudence have disappeared from the modern lexicon, undoubtedly a sign of the dehumanization of the man of today. Docility to whoever is familiar with reality in practical matters is also docility to what is real, both to situations in their variety and to the rule that assesses them and sees the connections among them. Docility is neither modesty nor humility, but the use

---

[29] In *ST*, II-II, q. 49, art. 4 Aquinas explains that *eustochia* is a part of prudence, and notes that it is a happy conjecture about any matter and that it is identified with shrewdness by Aristotle. [Tr.]
[30] *Nic. Eth.*, VI, 11, 1143b; Proverbs 23, 4; Ecclesiasticus 6, 35; *ST*, II-II, q. 49, art. 3, c and art. 4.

of the experience of others to reach, inasmuch as it is possible, a correct, and true understanding of a given situation. Docility is in this way the indispensable prelude to personal formation. Our inadequate memory and experience take on the riches that have accumulated in the memories and experience of others. Moreover, our prudence, in the process of formation, imitates the prudential actions of others who have already lived through the unpredictable difficulties of life and correctly dealt with contingencies, referring to principles for action and applying them to specific situations. This initiation into realism permits us to govern ourselves without ever losing contact with previous generations, to be enriched by them in turn and to transmit to generations after us the experience we have personally acquired. It is in this way, *and not otherwise*, that sound morals can continue, beyond the fleeting existence of individual morality in a society. It is in this way that man emerges from the barbarism characteristic of the state of nature to attain the state of civilization: through *tradition*, through the transmission of acquired moral capital that must be preserved at all costs, at the risk of rapidly falling back into the savagery proper to a nature that is undisciplined and left to itself. It is in this way that virtues, good habits that are not only personal but also *social*, are acquired, preserved, and transmitted over time.

We understand, then, why the indocility of generations, with their conflicts and divisions, always goes hand in hand with the idolatry of the "new

man" and the "new society." Nothing is more exhil-
arating than this venture, which panders to youth
with their unused, untapped energy. Yet nothing is
more chimerical. It is an attempt to remake a whole
civilization based on only one ready datum: the "I"
of each individual disconnected from any relationship with others, from recognized principles of moral
and social life, deprived of prudence, inebriated with
mythology by means of propaganda, becomes the prey
of leaders who, once raised to power, show him that
once the faculty of reason has been lost, the reasoning
of the strongest replaces practical reason and is always
shown to be the best.

V

THE COMMON GOOD AND POLITICAL PRUDENCE

RUDENCE IS THE QUEEN of a realm that it will never cease to explore: that of contingent realities, which rely on its clear-sightedness and governance. To order his conduct, the man beginning to exercise prudence has no other recourse than to refer to past contingent acts, deemed necessary when they were carried out. The only realities in moral matters that are clearly known to exist are *the human acts accomplished by others*, in which it can be observed, in the traces they have left behind them that they have *really* attained their proper end through means which have *really* proved themselves. *It is because prudence is a virtue involved in the social life of man that it is faithful to reality*. Without life in society, without a certain reciprocal influence of the behavior of members of society, prudence would not exist and the discovery of the golden mean or the suitable means would be left entirely to all the vicissitudes of chance circumstances and the subjective drives of man. In the exercise, perfection, and preservation of the virtue of prudence, we find that social bonds are present everywhere, the relations that unite men to each other as they pursue the same common good.

Prudence certainly always involves specific acts, yet it only correctly directs them toward their end if it imbues them with the universal nature of its theoretical framework: *recta ratio agibilium*. Prudence is undoubtedly creative, as it discovers the means appropriate for the *hic et nunc*, for this man here, and those specific circumstances there. But it does not create them starting from scratch. To discover how one must act in a given case is always to rediscover how others have acted in analogous cases, and to *adapt* the means they have used to the new situation in which one finds oneself. The ends of the moral life are eternal and immutable: justice always aims at rendering to each what is due him, fortitude at resisting the fear of death, temperance at taming the passions. How could the means not participate in the enduring relevance of the ends? The moral virtues did not come on the scene yesterday in the life of humanity, which in the course of the vicissitudes of history always draws near to perfection or distances itself from it. It is the same with prudence, its inseparable companion. The most ingenious, inventive man of prudence, richly endowed with resources, never departs from what has always been done in moral matters. He fine-tunes established practices, improving them, cutting away what is not pertinent. He makes a distinction between what is dead and what is living. The expression of Maurras, "true tradition is critical,"[1] is an aphorism of the prudent man.

The great majority of people act "as does the prudent man." For the prudent man is happy: *Beatitudo activa est actus prudentiae*,[2] that is, the happiness born of virtuous acts is the work of prudence. Aristotle writes, "If happiness lies in living and being active, and if the activity of the good man is virtuous and pleasant in itself," furthermore if "the fact that having a thing as our own is one of the attributes that make it pleasant for us, and if on the other hand we can contemplate those around us better than ourselves and their acts better than our own," then the man in search of happiness, as are all men, will never be solitary. He will need role models.[3] St. Thomas comments, "We can enjoy only what we know. But then if we know others better than ourselves, and their acts better than our own," because self-love always clouds our judgment of ourselves, we will always need the presence of happy, virtuous, and prudent persons around us who will show us the path to happiness.[4] Our prudence, the origin of our fortunate choices and our happiness, develops from our contact with prudent persons more advanced than we are and *becomes more objective, more grounded in reality* when we imitate them. This is why the prudent man is the measure of other men and their norm: *mensura unicuique homini*, for what is perfect in an order of

[1] *Mes idées politiques*, 1937. [Tr.]
[2] *On Virtue*, q. 1, art. 5, ad 8.
[3] *Nich. Eth.*, IX, 9, 1169b.
[4] *CNE*, 1896.

reality is precisely the standard pertaining to that order: what is great or small in it is measured by its proximity to or distance from that order, that is to say, from what is perfect in it. The prudent man is the very measure of the human race: *mensura in toto humano genere.*[5] He is the pivot upon whom society depends. It is not surprising to see that in the Middle Ages prudence was placed at the summit of the specifically human virtues. This is its natural place: it is the rule and measure of the true happiness of man.[6]

As the organizing center around which the moral life of a society is ordered, the prudent man is then the just man. It has not been observed, or very seldom in our opinion, that there is a close and even essential relationship between prudence and legal justice, which is entirely directed to the common good of society. It is however specifically highlighted in the work of Aristotle, in St. Thomas's commentaries, in the *Summa Theologiae* and elsewhere. Clearly neither the Stagirite nor the Angelic Doctor treated it extensively. The prudent man and the just man are one and the same for them. They seem to take this for granted: for Aristotle, there is no political society that is not founded on justice, the golden mean of which is established by prudence. For St. Thomas, as for St. Louis and the whole of medieval society, the *valiant* knight, the *prudent* knight gives an orientation to the social order where he establishes justice and imposes obedience to the law on all disturbers of the public peace.

---

[5] *CNE,* 1803 and 1905.
[6] *CNE,* 2062

Unity among citizens is the common good par excellence, and this unity is only possible if each renders unto others in society (*ad alium in communi*) what is due them. "A part, as such, belongs to a whole, so that the good of each part must be subordinated to the good of the whole. Thus the good of each virtue," those that concern us personally, such as fortitude and temperance, or those that concern others, such as distributive and commutative justice, "must be referred to the common good," to which legal justice subordinates us. Thus, all acts of virtue are able to be subsumed under legal justice, which subordinates man to the common good. "Since it pertains to the law to direct us to the common good, the justice that is termed general is called legal justice, since through it man submits to the law which directs all acts of virtue to the common good."[7] One could not put it better than to say that on one hand, legal justice is the driving force behind all the human virtues, just as "the sun which illumines and transforms all bodies by its presence . . . so does legal justice, inasmuch as it subordinates the acts of the other virtues to its own end, as it moves them by its command"[8]; on the other hand, the common good is constituted by the union of all who are bound to it through the subordination of many particular interests to the goal of unity.[9]

---

[7] In French *justice générale* is the term for legal justice, "which concerns what the citizen owes in fairness to the community," *CCC*, 2411. [Tr.] The source of the citation: *ST*, II-II, q. 58, art. 5, c.
[8] *ST*, II-II, q. 58, art. 6, c.
[9] See De Corte's *On Justice*.

St. Thomas's *Commentary on the Nicomachean Ethics* is equally explicit: there is no society without laws and there are no laws which are not aimed at the common good and which do not also "bid us carry out the deeds of a brave man (for example, not deserting one's post, not taking flight, not casting aside one's arms), those of a temperate man (for example, not committing adultery, not being insolent), those of a good-tempered man (like not striking others or speaking ill of them), and so on with regard to the other virtues and vices, prescribing some acts and forbidding others...This form of justice is then a complete virtue, though not absolutely but in our relations with others ... In justice every virtue can be found, as Euripides says."[10] St. Thomas adds that it is actually better to be perfect in relation to others than to be perfect with regard to oneself, since social relations give rise to many dimensions of perfection and thus render the virtue even more virtuous. We must then conclude that union as perfect as possible with others and with the common good is virtue at its highest point of perfection: *est virtus maxime perfecta*,[11] and that "according to Bias, one of the seven wise men of Greece, the use of authority reveals the man, because he who rules is connected to others and it pertains to him to order all things to the common good."[12] Consequently "the most perfect man is not the one who practices his virtue only in relation to

[10] *Nic. Eth.*, V, 1, 1129b and *CNE*, 900–906.
[11] *CNE*, 907.
[12] *CNE*, 909.

himself, but also in relation to others."[13] St. Thomas comments on *sed etiam ad alterum* with *sed etiam ad amicos*,[14] because legal justice is the principle of unity and thus of friendship among citizens.[15]

It is clear that if the perfect man is just and if he is prudent, then the just man and the prudent man are one and the same man, who has come to the point of human perfection. Furthermore, we know that the *imperium*, government, pertains to prudence. He who governs with the goal of the common good that is greater than his own good and his inferiors' must then be prudent, his justice one and the same with his prudence. As perfect virtues acting in all virtues, justice and prudence are the two aspects of the most perfect virtuous action which man can carry out here below. This is why the ancient symbol represented prudence as *Janus bifrons*,[16] or also as an arrow with a serpent wrapped around it.[17] A further explanation came later: On the one hand, "legal justice is not a particular virtue in the strict sense of the word, but a virtue to which all virtue is connected."[18] On the other hand, all virtuous acts are subject to deliberation, to the decision and command of prudence. Ergo, there is no point of real difference between justice and prudence, only a difference in understanding.

[13] *Nic. Eth.* V, 1, 1130a.
[14] Respectively "but also with regard to others" and "but also with regard to friends." [Tr.]
[15] *CNE*, 910.
[16] Two-faced Janus. [Tr.]
[17] The serpent represents wisdom and the arrow justice. [Tr.]
[18] *CNE*, 911.

This is what St. Thomas strongly affirms: *pruden-tia et politica sunt idem habitus secundum substantiam, quia utraque est recta ratio rerum agibilium circa humana bona et mala*, that is, prudence and politics form only one habit in terms of their essence, since both rationally and justly determine how to act in matters related to good or evil. They differ logically (*secundum rationem*) in that prudence refers to what is good or bad for the individual, while politics deals with what is good or bad for society. Yet as the actions of the individual always have a direct or indirect social effect, as a function of the subordination of the part to the whole, it follows that prudence in the broad sense of the word is political prudence, *prudencia architectonica*,[19] which regulates all of human life.[20]

This is confirmed by the express declaration of St. Thomas, in his commentary on the first book of Aristotle's *Nicomachean Ethics*, concerning the archi-tectonic nature of politics (*scientia civilis*),[21] which, as such, orders all of human life toward it final end, and *principalissime*,[22] the common good of the state.[23] Maurras is compellingly right to declare "Politics first," since it concerns the earthly destiny of man. The *scientia civilis architectonica* and the *prudentia architectonica* are obviously identical. Legal justice, an essential virtue for the political man concerns

[19] Architectonic in the sense of providing direction; this is the same as political prudence. [Tr.]
[20] *CNE*, 1196–1199.
[21] Political science. [Tr.]
[22] Most importantly. [Tr.]
[23] *CNE*, 25 and 1197.

universaliter[24] all aspects of moral life (*circa totam materiam moralem*),[25] as prudence, the good counselor, concerns everything related to human life (*ad totam vitam*).[26]

Political prudence, in which the highest and noblest virtues come together, joining forces and essentially fusing into one, is the human virtue par excellence.

As usual, St. Thomas relies on Aristotle to establish the basis for this. We are gravely mistaken, he says, following the Stagirite, in thinking that the prudent man is one who is only concerned about himself and his own affairs, since each individual person cannot fruitfully pursue his own good if his prudential reasoning concerning this particular good is not aligned with the common good.[27] Too often the reason put forward for this error is that man cannot and must not look for anything other than his own good. "But this opinion is contrary to charity, which does not seek its own advantage . . . and to right reason, which judges the common good to be better than the good of one individual." "When one seeks the common good of the many, he consequently seeks his own good. First, because one's own good cannot exist without the common good of the family, state, or kingdom . . . Then, since man, as a member of his household and the state, must consider what is good for him relative to the good of the many, as the good

---

[24] Without exception. [Tr.]

[25] *CNE*, 919.

[26] *CNE*, 1163.

[27] *Nic. Eth.*, VI, 8, 1142; *CNE*, 1205–1206.

disposition of parts depends on their relation to the whole." To whoever would counter that temperance and fortitude, which are ruled by prudence, are to be understood only in relation to one's own good, at which point prudence has a role, we must answer that those virtues come under the law and also concern the common good. Moreover, "prudence and justice are directly related to it, since they belong to the rational faculty: the common good also pertains to reason, while the pursuit of an individual good has to do with the faculty of the senses."[28] Political prudence thus imitates the prudence — or providence — of God, which is extended to the common good of the world of which He is the master.[29]

This is why prudence, a virtue of the intellect, is found in its most eminent degree in the Prince, whose function is to intelligently govern the multitude, directing them to the common good. This type of prudence in no way pertains to the subject qua subject, whose proper function is to be directed and governed, but it pertains to him, as a rational being, in the degree to which he participates in the life of the state, and, endowed with a free will, chooses to obey the law rather than to break it. In this respect he, in turn, has his own kind of political prudence. To put it another way, political prudence is in the mind of the Prince like the plans for a house are

[28] Here the "faculty of the senses" undoubtedly refers not to the five external senses, but to the interior senses, consciousness, imagination, instinct, and memory. [Tr.] *ST*, II-II, q. 47, art. 10, c. and ad 2 and 3.
[29] *ST*, I, q. 22, art. 1, c.

in the mind of an architect, and like the project of the construction of the house, conformed to those plans, is in the mind and hands of the mason.[30] As architectonic art is to the subordinate manual arts, the political prudence of the head is to that of the subject. The subject's rational discernment regarding the common good of the society to which he belongs is thus determined by his *actual* position in the state and the *actual* services he renders to it. *Real* service to the common good is the *real* measure of political prudence. The greater the position one *actually* holds within the state, the more political prudence obliges him to *really* serve society, and vice versa.

Honed by *effectively* seeking the common good that transcends all individual goods, *political prudence* considers the means most suited to this end, chooses the one which is appropriate in the case at hand, and orders its implementation—*the highest human virtue*. Nothing surpasses the virtue that St. Thomas calls *royal prudence* (*prudentia regnativa*), "seated in one who has to govern not only himself, but the whole of society in a city or kingdom ... and so prudence in its most perfect sense belongs to a king." "This is why," St. Thomas adds, "the execution of justice, part of the royal office, as it is ordered to the common good also stands in need of the guidance of prudence." He concludes by associating these two virtues at their apex: thus prudence and justice "belong most properly to a king," but "since governance pertains rather to a king and execution to his subjects, kingly prudence,

---

[30] *ST*, II-II, q. 47, art. 12, c and q. 50, art. 2, c. and ad 2.

reckoned as a kind of prudence, has to do with governance rather than justice, which concerns execution."[31]
This is understandable as prudence is a virtue of the
intellect that "consists in applying thinking to action,
which is effected by the will,"[32] and "which is not
done without rectitude of the appetite."[33] The intellect is always superior to the will. Political prudence
is the pinnacle of all the human virtues.

We see this when we look at the potential parts
of prudence: *euboulia*, *synesis*, and *gnome*, which are
associated with prudence and ordered to its acts or
to preliminary or secondary matters which fall under
the governance of prudence.

"Deliberation (*euboulia* in Greek) implies an inquiry
on the part of reason about actions to be performed
and *in which human life consists* (*in quibus consistit
vita humana*)."[34] "Since deliberation is ordered to
command, which is the principle act, it is similarly
ordered toward prudence, which is the principle virtue, without which it would not even be a virtue."[35]
If *euboulia* bears on everything having to do with
human life, what can we say then about political
prudence, for which *euboulia* prepares the action
of imposing the observation of the law on others?

Judgment (or *synesis*), which refers to correct judgment, not in speculative matters but in the arena
of individual actions, is even more excellent than

[31] *ST*, II-II, q. 50, art. 1.
[32] *ST*, II-II, q. 47, art. 1, ad 3.
[33] *ST*, II-II, q. 47, art. 4, c.
[34] *ST*, II-II, q. 51, art. 1, c.
[35] *ST*, II-II, q.51, art. 2.

deliberation. There are those who easily conceptualize the greatest range of acts to be performed, who discuss them brilliantly, weighing the pros and the cons, but who do not have the ability to judge correctly. They are full of good advice, but they do not have the ability to judge a thing exactly as it is (*secundum quod in se est*). *Synesis* has the task of emptying the mind of mistaken concepts, pipe dreams, and utopian projects, and by means of good judgment to go straight to the *realistic* solution, the one which corresponds not only to the universal principles relevant to the act, but also to the particular means through which the intended virtuous end can be attained. In communicating its objectivity to the governance belonging to political prudence, *good judgment* allows it to properly order what must be done in a particular case "toward the one final end, which is living the whole of life well," of which the common good is the perfect form here below.[36]

It is the same with *gnome*, which makes good judgment more perspicacious and better oriented to reality in that it knows what must or must not be done in a situation, which, under accepted norms, would end up with the wrong solution, but which, enlightened by loftier principles, is correctly resolved. The classic example is that you must not give back to an enemy of the fatherland something entrusted to you, the restitution of which would be harmful to the common good. The realism of political prudence is refined here, rendered more robust, stringent, and rigorous. Thus, the penetrating power of *gnome* enriches political

[36] *ST*, II-II, q. 51, art. 3, c. and ad 1; see also art. 2, ad 2.

prudence and likens it to divine providence, whose gaze extends over everything which could happen in the world outside the normal course of events.[37]

With its way prepared by the virtues of counsel, good judgment, and perspicacity, political prudence is the most excellent type of prudence since the end to which its action is ordered is the most eminent envisaged by man. Beyond this end, there is only the vision of God, the gratuitous gift of the divine generosity and the universal common good in the supernatural order. The proper object of political prudence is thus: *the law which prescribes the way in which men living in society can strive for the common good and achieve unity, harmony, and peace, without which no civilization is possible. Recta ratio se habet ad appetitum rectum sicut motivum et regula extrinseca*: correct prudential reasoning functions as the motive and the extrinsic norm which directs the will which is aligned to the good, and in this case to the common good. It is like the charioteer who directs his chariot towards the finish line.[38] The definition of the law as "an ordinance of reason promulgated in view of the common good by the one in charge of the community" is a clear statement of this.[39] A politics in which the law serves as a means to the common good is the ultimate temporal end of man.

This means that there is no morality which is not subordinated to the common good. This means that

[37] *ST*, II-II, q. 51, art. 4, c. and ad e.
[38] *CNE*, 327.
[39] *ST*, I-II, q. 90, art. 4, c.

the right term for morality is politics. Aristotle and St. Thomas never cease to state forcefully that politics is the practical foundational science par excellence from which all human conduct draws its meaning. By authentic politics is meant politics actually conformed to the rational animal whose sole objective is: *to become what he is.* The human intellect, whether speculative or practical, has no other object.

The characteristic feature of law, good law, is to make men virtuous: *legislatores assuefaciendo homines per praecepta, praemia et poenas ad opera virtutum, faciunt eos virtuosos. Et ad hoc debet fieri intentio cuiuslibet legislatoris. Qui vero hoc non bene faciunt peccant in legislatione. Et horum civilitas differt a recta civilitate secundum differentiam boni et mali.*[40] This could not be affirmed more forcefully. If the intention of the legislator neglects this end, then the state, the seat of civilization, which he directs will be anything but a state, and consequently not a civilization ordered to the common good of human life. There will then no longer be a life which can properly be called human.

It is not the case that the law affects each individual act of man. St. Thomas, who recognizes the primacy of

---

[40] *CNE*, 251. [By means of precepts, rewards, and punishments, legislators make men virtuous by habituating them to virtuous works. This should be the aim of every legislator. Indeed, he who does not succeed in this fails in lawmaking. It is in this way that a good manner of government differs from a bad one. (Tr.)] One should read the entire Treatise on Law [*ST*, I-II, q. 90–108], which is a long commentary on our text. See also M. De Corte, "Telle est la Loi," *Itinéraires*, no. 127, November, 1968.

political prudence—*Lex positiva dicitur architectonica prudentia*[41]—gives a place to "monastic," or personal, prudence,[42] to which he assigns care to obey the law, as we have emphasized above. But the law, even positive law, always continues to play an important role in morality, on the condition that it refer back to the natural law, that it conform to human nature, and, even more important, that it depend on the eternal law and the God-given order showing forth over the whole universe. Once again we see how *Aristotelian and Thomistic morality, far from being a morality of the individual* (introduced by a Christianity that has lost its moorings and publicly prescribed since Kant), *is a political matter.* How could it be otherwise, then, within a perspective which subordinates the part to the whole in line with the most striking evidence and a realism completely founded on reason?

It does not take an informed observer to observe that right before our eyes most people are not obedient to what their reason dictates, as the prudent man is, but to legal constraints. In practical matters, the goal, that is, the common good, totally oriented to what is truly human, does not consist of purely theoretical study and knowledge about various kinds of actions, *but rather in carrying them* out: *finis scientiae quae est circa operabilia non est cognoscere et speculari singula, sicut in scientiis speculativis, sed magis facere*

---

[41] *CNE*, 1197. [Positive law is called architectonic [or legislative] prudence. (Tr.)]

[42] This is prudence directed to one's own good. See *ST*, II-II, q. 47, art. II, c. [Tr.]

ipsa.[43] It is not enough to know what prudence is, and how it works, it must be possessed and put into practice. According to Aristotle, experience tells us that arguments influence only generous souls possessed of moral nobility, but are powerless to motivate the majority of people to lead a noble, honest life. The masses, in fact, do not naturally obey through an appeal to honor, but only out of fear of punishment. Dominated by passions, people pursue their own pleasures and the means to attain them, and avoid penalties opposed to these pleasures. They have no idea about what is noble and truly pleasant, since they have never experienced this. For persons like this, what argument could transform their nature? In general, passion yields not to reasoning, but to force.[44] For the person who tenaciously holds principles contrary to the common good, there is no other recourse save the force of law established by the underlying prudence of the political leader.[45] The law here takes the place of prudence for those who have none. It directs their will just as prudence orders the means to the end in the virtuous man. In other words, obedience to the law for the majority of people is the necessary substitute for prudence; without this no society would be possible.

But this obedience is not the result of mere force. As the remarkable proverb has it, *it makes virtue of necessity*. Aristotle and St. Thomas insist on this with striking good sense; most of those in a position of

---

[43] *CNE*, 2138.
[44] *Nic. Eth.*, X, 9, 1179 and *CNE*, 2141.
[45] *CNE*, 2142–2147.

authority in no matter what domain have lost even the memory of this: to receive from one's youth an education rightly oriented to virtue is difficult to imagine when one has not been brought up *under just laws*, for to live with temperance and perseverance is not pleasant for most people, especially when they are young. Thus, it is important to use legal means to regulate the manner in which they are educated as well as the kind of life they should live, which will no longer be painful when it has become habitual. This observation holds for man's entire life.[46] *Ad hoc indigemus legibus, et non solum a principio, quando scilicet aliquis incipit fieri vir, sed etiam universaliter per totam vitam hominis.*[47] The law has an essentially educational value: its end is to make men virtuous. This is impossible if the lives of people are not directed by an intellect which has a conception of order conducive to the good, and the coercive power to compel the recalcitrant. And as a father does not possess this authority any more than does any prudent man whatsoever, there remains only the prince armed with the power of the law. The law is the prudential instruction (*sermo procedens ab aliqua prudentia et intellectus*) which orients human acts towards the good. It follows that the law is necessary to make men good.[48] It is not burdensome (*non est onerosa, gravis vel odiosa*[49]) if it requires all people to lead a virtuous life.[50]

[46] *Nic. Eth.*, X, 9, 1179–1180.
[47] *CNE*, 2150.
[48] *CNE*, 2153.
[49] It is not oppressive, burdensome, or odious. [Tr.]
[50] *CNE*, 2154.

No matter what man is charged with legislating and enforcing the law, if this task falls to anyone, it is most certainly to the man with practical knowledge, as is the case in medicine and in anything involving the services and prudence of others.[51] This knowledge encompasses discernment about everything that fosters life in a community (*scientia communium*) and permits the one so endowed, enlightened by the principle of the common good, to embrace the particular means which will strengthen the community, in line with his practical experience in political matters. No one can become a statesman just by living an ordinary life in a well-ordered state. Organizing empiricism, study, and political experience, this latter based on knowledge of the past and the very nature of reality, are of utmost importance.[52] Without this indissoluble alliance between doctrine and its application, between theory and practice, politics falls outside the scope of prudence, which prescribes tested means, or those which it devises taking those means as a model, directed to the common good, the unchanging essence of every human society. We can never say it too often: *In practical matters, where action is directed to an end, prudence is queen.*

Everything else is literary invention, fiction, a work of the imagination. Yet we know today that the novel is not in competition with the civil state, but with practical knowledge concerning the government of societies. Nothing is easier than building an imagined, perfect society in the clouds and to employ rhetoric

[51] *Nic. Eth.*, X, 9, 1180b.
[52] *CNE*, 2171.

to spread the mirage abroad in the souls of those whose social bonds have been broken and who aspire with every mutilated fiber of their being to the society which they have lost. This has been observed by Aristotle and confirmed by St. Thomas: "The sophists who boast that they teach political science are clearly far off the mark. They do not know what its nature is, not what its object is: *otherwise they would not have mistaken rhetoric for political science.* They would not have considered that legislating is an easy thing, reducing it to the mere collection of laws approved by public opinion. The selection of these is a work of the intellect (*synesis*), and here prudential discernment is essential. One would never become a doctor by simply studying compendia of prescriptions."[53]

Collections of laws and constitutions are only useful to those capable of reflecting on them and discovering what is good or bad in them and what kinds of legal provisions are suited to a given situation. They lose all value in the hands of those without political experience.[54] *Omnia haec videntur esse utilia solis expertis, illis autem qui nesciunt singularia propter inexperientiam videntur esse inutilia.*[55]

We keep coming back to the same point: "to complete the philosophy of what is human" (*hé peri ta anthrôpeia philosophia*),[56] that is to say "knowledge

---

[53] *Nic. Eth.*, X, 9, 1181a and *CNE*, 2172–2177.
[54] *Nic. Eth.*, X, 9, 1181b.
[55] *CNE*, 2177. [All this is seen to be useful only to those with experience, but is useless to those who are ignorant of particulars due to their own inexperience. (Tr.)]
[56] *Nic. Eth.* X, 9, 1181b.

about what to do (*scientia operativa*), which is concerned with what is human (*quae est circa humana*)," we must have recourse to *political prudence*. This virtue assembles as much information as possible on laws and constitutions, past and present. It then proceeds to an examination of monarchy, rule by the aristocracy, and republics, and of their corrupted forms, tyranny, oligarchy, and democracy.[57] It strives to discover "what kinds of influences preserve or destroy states and particular kinds of constitutions, and due to which causes some states are well-governed and others just the opposite." This is the stage where political prudence is operative. "It can then better discern which is the best of constitutions." At this juncture, prudence makes a decision. It determines "which laws and customs each constitution must make use of" in order to assure the common good. This is the decisive step for the *imperium*,[58] when the highest of the human virtues completes its work.[59]

The foundational virtue of prudence thus establishes a state in which the laws incarnate the principle of synderesis, without which no reasoning about morality is possible and men act randomly, with no end in mind. "One must do good and avoid evil." The moral order depends on the political order which, for the vast throng, is its cause. These lack the ability, the desire, and the time to reason correctly to attain their true good. Good governance of men is the only way

[57] See Aristotle's *Politics*. [Tr.]
[58] Here, government. [Tr.]
[59] *Nic. Eth.*, X, 9, 1181b and *CNE*, 2179–2180.

to arrive at good self-governance for the majority of
rational animals. Once again, we must appreciate how
profound this basic human requirement is: *politics
first*. It is not just that this should come first in time,
anticipating an order of higher *human* values, such
as a civilization, and providing for its foundation. It
is a matter of primacy in the order of *causes*: politics
encompasses all man's activities and endows them
with *human* significance. As its name indicates,[60] true
civilization depends on politics, i.e., correct politics,
which is the work of prudence. Justice itself, i.e., correct justice, that strives for the common good and renders to each what is due him in accord with the level
of service he provides to society, simple egalitarian
justice relating to material exchanges,[61] will in turn
flourish only in a society ruled by political prudence.
Personal morality thrives only with the warmth and
enlightenment provided by political prudence. The
virtues that perfect each person develop only within
a well-ordered society, as well-ordered as possible,
in which prudence constantly reveals the means to
preserve the common good and unity among all. St.
Thomas emphatically asserts: "It is impossible for a
man to be good unless he is properly related to the
common good," *impossibile est quod aliquis homo sit
bonus, nisi sit bene proportionatus bono communi.*[62]
"Man must consider what is good for himself based on

---

[60] The word "politics" is derived from *polis*, Greek for city; the
term "civilization" is derived from the Latin *civilis*, civil, and is
related to *civitas*, city. [Tr.]
[61] This is more commonly referred to as distributive justice. [Tr.]
[62] *ST*, I-II, q. 92, art. 1, ad 3.

what is prudent with respect to the common good," *oportet quod homo consideret quid sit sibi bonum ex hoc quod est prudens circa bonum multitudinis.*[63] One cannot be virtuous without being a good citizen. "It is proper to the law to lead subjects to the acquisition of their own virtue. Then, since virtue makes the one who possesses it good, it follows that the proper effect of law" — an act of political prudence — "is to make those to whom it is given good."[64]

Such is the political body where prudence is the queen: it is "the Catholic ark, classical, hierarchical, *human*, where ideas are not empty words, nor institutions inconsistent illusions, nor laws banalities, nor governments, plunderers and bad managers." It is in this state where in spite of all its human failings there is manifest "the invisible primacy of Order and the Good."[65] It is this state that ensures the natural happiness of man. "The final temporal achievement of man is not found on the steppes or in forests. It is attained through the universal sharing in all the goods which a well-ordered society is in a position to offer man. In this way, in the order of practical accomplishments, the state emerges as having the potential to be highly efficacious, as the only entity able to provide for human welfare with a certain measure of completeness."[66]

---

[63] *ST*, II-II, q. 47, art. 10, ad 2.
[64] *ST*, I-II, q. 92, art. 1.
[65] Charles Maurras, *De la politique naturelle au nationalism intégral*, selected texts, edited by F. Natter and C. Rousseau, Paris, 1972, p. 277.
[66] L. Lachance, *L'humanisme politique de saint Thomas d'Aquin*, Paris, 1965.

Beatitudo activa est actus prudentiae.[67] The happiness born of human acts is the work of political prudence, the most human of all the virtues. Political prudence is the *habitus* that governs all the other virtues and orders them to the final end of man here on earth: *habitus qui ordinatur ad finem ultimum et imperat allis habitibus.*[68]

How is it then, that such a virtue has disappeared today, to the point where no mention of it is made in common moral codes, nor in the Church, charged with preserving it, nor in politics? If the term for it has been lost, how can we get it back? If we no longer know the final end to which we here below are destined, if we have lost the key to happiness, are we not constrained to create a replacement, an imaginary key which will then only be able to open sham locks and set us out on illusory paths that lead nowhere? Are we not then condemned to perpetual unhappiness?

Such is the adventure of the human species ever since the Renaissance. If our world today is placed under the banner of *technology* and a totally industrialized civilization, unprecedented in history, and is in the process of extending itself over the whole planet, it is precisely because there is no substitute for prudence, which has vanished; only technical skill remains.

---

[67] Active happiness is an act of prudence. [Tr.]
[68] *On Virtue*, q. 1, art. 5, ad 8.

VI
ART AND TECHNIQUE

HIS TRIUMPH OF TECHNI-
cal skill, art in the most general sense
of the term, over prudence is facilitated
by the fact that it is, like prudence, a
virtue of the practical intellect and that
the intellect of man, united to his body, is so to speak
constrained to carry out the operations of political
prudence in institutions and law, as *creations* of the
human genius designed to respond to given situations.
The indeterminate character of the object of the prudential act has need of supplementation from *art* in
order to make specific determinations to serve as a
framework or channel for subsequent operations of
prudence confronted with new situations.

Thus, it is important to determine, as precisely as
possible, the nature of art and especially to emphasize
its subordination to prudence as a function of this
virtue's fully human character.

Art is defined as the ability to produce an *artefactum,* that is, to impose on matter apt to receive it a
determining form, a structure conceptualized by the
mind. The *artefactum*, the product of art, is something *which can be made*, fashioned, shaped by man

according to a predetermined design. It is a *factibile*.[1]
It can exist or not. It depends on what its author has
decreed. It is thus radically contingent. Its existence
depends on someone who has the know-how[2] to
make it, to *produce* it, to engender it as something
outside himself. For this reason, art is defined as the
recta ratio factibilium, that is, the correct determination of things to be made, the technical knowledge of
the transformation of creatures and things.[3] Causality
in art is essentially based on an exemplar: the image
or mental representation of the object to be made
or the thing to be reshaped is the principle for the
work to be carried out by the artisan. This is what
the plans for a house are in the mind of the architect,
and the result of his action is the resemblance of the
house to the design.[4] In other words, everything that
involves making things presupposes the union of
speculative knowledge and the activity of creating:
*ratio humana eorum quae sunt secundum artem est
cognoscitiva, id est speculativa, et factiva.*[5] "The artisan
first perceives the mental representation of a house
in a fully developed way and then realizes it in the
material": *artifex primo apprehendit formam domus
absolute et postea inducit eam in materia.*"[6]

[1] Something which it is possible to make. [Tr.]
[2] De Corte adds "know how" in English to supplement the
French phrase. [Tr.]
[3] *On Virtue*, q. 1, art. 7, c; *ST*, I-II, q. 56, art. 3, c. and q. 57,
art. 3, c., art. 4, c. and art. 5 ad 1; *CNE*, 316; *Commentary on
Aristotle's Metaphysics*, I, no. 34.
[4] *ST*, I, q. 15, art. 1, c and art. 3, c.
[5] Aquinas, *Commentary on Aristotle's Politics*, I, Prologue, 2.
[6] Aquinas, *Commentary on Aristotle's On the Heavens*, I, Prologue, 2.

In this sense, the knowledge man has about making things resembles the creative knowledge of God, which bears not only upon the universal form of each creature, but also on the matter which differentiates it, and extends to the knowledge of individual beings in their very uniqueness. If the technician with his knowledge could produce an object in the completeness of its being, and not just in its ideal form, this knowledge would be divine. Like God, the artisan creates objects which exist in reality: while God creates the being that exists right down to root of its substantial existence (*esse simpliciter*), the artisan only produces a new state for one or another particular thing (*esse hoc*),[7] a result of the transformative power which he possesses. To put it even more precisely, while God is purely and simply the creator of existence (*esse*), and knows each individual being more profoundly and radically than it could ever know itself, the artisan is the cause of an object's becoming transformed (*fieri*) into an *esse hoc*, one or another concrete thing of which the artisan knows the ideal form from his intellect, which is the cause of it. He can only know it in its uniqueness through his senses, since he is not the cause of the matter which individualizes the form and which existed before his work.[8] To know something is really to know its cause.

We must deduce from this that the knowledge of making things, or "poetic" knowledge,[9] implies

[7] *Summa Contra Gentiles*, II, 2 and III, 66; Aquinas, *Disputed Questions on the Power of God*, q. 5 art. 1, ad 5.
[8] *ST,* I, q. 104, art. 1, c.; q. 90, art. 3; and q. 105, art. 2, ad 3.
[9] In the sense of the Greek verb *poiein*, to make, fashion, work, construct, produce a work external to the agent.

knowledge which contemplates mental images of "things to be made," which do not actually yet exist when their creator thinks of them. It is not knowledge of *that which is*, like speculative knowledge, knowledge of the essences or natures which exist independently of us, but rather knowledge of *that by which* a particular thing can exist in virtue of our creative decision. It does not know the *quod* but the *quo*.[10] The architect does not know the house he builds in the way that the astronomer knows the sky that he contemplates. He knows the house because he knows the plans *by which* he is going to construct it, and these mental plans are the equivalent of the nature or essence of the house that is built. The *quo* is the substitute of the *quod* in the architect's thought. For him knowing means knowing the means, techniques, know-how, method, processes, formulas, instruments, tools, machines, skills, tricks of the trade, maneuvers, expedient measures, mechanisms, tactics, strategies, in short, everything *through which* a thing created by man comes into existence. To know that is to know the thing itself, the *factibile*.[11]

Let us note that this knowledge presupposes man's total submission to the matter into which he introduces his mental representations. The transformation of matter by man and the concomitant spirit of domination over this matter necessarily entail submission to what is most indeterminate in an entity: the shapeless material which will receive

[10] "What" and "by which" respectively. [Tr.]
[11] What can be made. [Tr.]

its form from the intellect operating on it. "We cannot command Nature except by obeying her," said Bacon.[12] The Hegelian dialectic of master and slave is borne out here to a much greater degree than in the domain of the social. The man who is victorious over matter is always losing himself in it. If in order to know a thing one must make it, the order of knowledge is reversed: the external world no longer becomes a mental reality as a result of being thought of; it is thought which is materialized in order to become known.

Prudence, which is concerned with the particular and the contingent just like art, is fundamentally different from it. The mental attitude towards the *agibilia*[13] is profoundly different from the mental attitude towards the *factibilia*. Prudence orders man to act *correctly* as he exercises virtuous *habitus* which make him good, perfecting him. It deliberates, makes choices, commands. It is the principle of internal operations which leave their trace in man, making his conduct more virtuous, making him more of a man. Moreover it is obvious that "all the *agibilia* have their being in the one who accomplishes them" and nowhere else. On the contrary, "craftsmanship has as its object the things which are makeable, that is, which are produced using external matter, like a house, a knife, and other similar things."[14] The

---

[12] *Novum Organum* (1620) by Francis Bacon (1561–1626), English philosopher and statesman.

[13] Things that can be done, as opposed to *factibilia*, things which can be made. [Tr.]

[14] *ST*, II-II, q. 47, art. 5, c; I-II, q. 57, art. 4, c.

artisan's object is the perfection of the object he is
making, while the object of prudence is the perfecting
of the agent himself.[15] Prudence is an internal activity
while craftsmanship works on an object.

Let us note the fact that the internal activity of
prudence has nothing subjective about it. Prudence
does not perfect the subject as one walled within his
subjectivity. It perfects him as one endowed with a
practical intellect, the faculty that comprehends the
contingent just as the speculative intellect does: in
being conformed to reality and to the truth which it
possesses, *secundum eandem rationem objecti, scilicet
secundum rationem entis et veri*,[16] without letting the
alleged demands of the subject affect the objectivity
of the intellect, but on the contrary anchoring it in
the true and the good as is its responsibility. The
contingent action commanded by prudence obviously does not have the same objective coherence
as the necessary truths that sustain the speculative
intellect. It must conform to the subject's will, rendered upright, but this rectification of the will is
strictly dependent on the final end, which is perforce imposed on the appetite, which is free, under
the form of the Sovereign Good. There is nothing
contingent, as St. Thomas often repeats, which is
not ballasted with necessity.

We can even propose without contradiction that
craftsmanship that aims at the perfection of the
object produced rather than at the perfection of the

[15] *ST*, I-II, q. 57, art. 5, ad 1; q. 56, art. 5, ad 2.
[16] *ST*, I, q. 79, art. 8, ad 3.

creator has much more to do with the subject than the object. By making things, man expresses himself subjectively as he has before him matter which he transforms, adapting it to his needs. The surroundings in which he finds himself are then modified, with the result that the metamorphosis effected by the artisan is useful or pleasant to him. This is why the art of making things is ordered to specific ends, contrary to prudence, which is "of good counsel about matters which pertain to the whole of man's life and the final end of human life," *de his quae pertinent ad totam vitam hominis et ad ultimum finem vitae humanae.*[17] The artisanal (or poetic) intellect is restricted to domains differing from each other as a function of the various needs which the human subject aspires to meet in order to assure his survival. "Nature has provided food for animals, coats of fur, means of defense such as teeth, horns, claws, or at least a means of rapid flight. Man, on the other hand, has been created without being provided by nature with anything similar. Instead, though, he has been given the *power of reasoning* which enables him to fashion all these things *with his hands.*"[18] Reason, the faculty concerned with what is universal, which influences techniques, causes them to be specialized according to the privations which the individual endures from birth and which he attempts to palliate to keep on living. There is no Technique which concerns man in his totality. Technique with

[17] *ST*, I-II, q. 57, art. 4, ad 3.
[18] Aquinas, *On the Governance of Rulers*, I, 1.

an upper-case "T" is a myth that does not stand
up to analysis. There are only techniques aimed at
particular ends. Technique can never in any way be
"architectonic" like prudence in view of its constitutive tendency to specialize. It follows that technical
methods provide various kinds of *tools* which man
lacks, without which he can ensure neither his own
survival nor, consequently, that of the species. *The
tools are for his use.* They are *useful* to him.

When they are termed useful this means that they
are useful to the man who employs the technical
methods in question or has others employ them for
his purposes. *Finis ultimus cujuslibet facientis, in
quantum facientis, est ipsemet; utimur enim factis
a nobis propter nos,* that is, the ultimate end of any
producer, inasmuch as he is the producer, is himself; everything that we make is for our own sake.[19]
*Nos sumus fines omnium artificialium; omnia enim
propter hominis usum fiunt,* that is, we are the end
of everything that is made; all that is made is for
man's use,[20] whether he himself makes things or
uses others as intermediaries. All man's efforts to
dominate the world through technology are ordered
to himself inasmuch as he is a subject endowed with
the instinct of self-preservation. The perfection of
the object made according to specific technical norms
has as its end the subject who fashions it. Its being
and its existence as an object refer back to the being
and existence of the subject, of which they are the

---

[19] *Summa Contra Gentiles*, III, 17.
[20] *Summa Contra Gentiles*, III, 36.

extension. Nothing is more closely connected to the subjectivity of man than the objects he manufactures. We can understand it thus: the making of things is an effect, the cause of which lies entirely in man himself, the material cause excepted.[21] The work bears the stamp of man. It is marked with his image. It formally[22] depends on the thought of man, evident in the work, as it is so to speak poured out onto the matter of the object, so much so that the technician only encounters himself in the world that he subjects to his needs. He is not dependent on the world he fashions, with the exception of matter; he conforms the world to the idea he has formed of it. This is the very definition of idealism, starting with Descartes and Kant. The world is identified with my will and the representation I make of it. While prudence is realistic, the making of things, taken as such, is idealistic. As a result, all idealistic philosophies are poetry and not philosophy. They are all creations of the mind, works of art, novels, literature, often quite poor.

If a work of art, in both the broad and narrow sense of the term,[23] depends on the inventive intellect of its author, it must be said that art is a more purely intellectual virtue than prudence, whose action is never

[21] The material cause refers to the matter out of which a thing is made. [Tr.]

[22] That is to say, according to the formal cause of the object, which depends on a mental concept of man. It refers to the form or shape that the matter takes on. [Tr.]

[23] For St. Thomas and Aristotle the narrow sense of the term refers to the making of things. [Tr.]

disassociated from the moral virtues, the exercise of which sets prudence on the right course. This is why the artist can voluntarily sin against his art without ceasing to be an artist, while the prudent person can never intentionally commit an error in his deliberation, judgment, or conduct without ceasing to be prudent. Aristotle notes that the artist who deliberately makes an error in art is held to be a better artist than one who does so unknowingly, since the technique of the latter is obviously lacking. It is the same with those who knowingly use incorrect grammar compared to those who are ignorant of grammar. But it is not the same with prudence: the one who willingly sins against prudence receives less praise than one who does so without willing it. We can say the same about moral virtues that are sinned against: where there is no will to sin, there is no sin. This is the case because prudence implies an appetite which is well-ordered with regard to the virtuous end in sight. We thus see clearly that prudence cannot be confused with art, which has the task of making the work correspond to the model elaborated by the mind. Like the moral virtues prudence requires an upright appetite.[24] This is why a technique does not make the one who uses it good. It makes him a good technician and not a man in the full sense of the word. For there to be good use of art, something else is required.[25] Prudence and

[24] *CNE*, 1173.
[25] *ST*, I-II, q. 57, art. 3, ad 1. [The text De Corte refers to reads: "[Art] falls short of being a perfect virtue because it does not result in good usage; for this something else is required." (Tr.)]

the moral virtues are necessary, personal prudence, prudence in economics, prudence in military strategy, and especially political prudence,[26] which reveals the means of integrating into the common good of the polity the useful goods which are the product of man's adroit genius and which are destined for his use according to the common good of the polity without their private character threatening the most valuable of human goods: unity. In addition, justice is necessary, "which makes the artisan's will upright and inclines him to do his work conscientiously."[27] Justice also prompts individuals, whose principle concern is their livelihood, to reconcile their own interests with their essential duty to serve the common good, which, moreover, assures that these interests will be protected.

It is by the subordination of the artisan's work to practical reason that it acquires moral significance. Without this subordination, he only has skills analogous to what all animals have in order to defend, ensure, protect, and shore up their existence, without any value which could be called human, so to speak. All art, no matter of what kind, is inhuman if it is not imbued with prudence. We feel shame when we bring to mind evidence of an age in which the loss of the sense of what is human leads man to endlessly transform the world, to subject it to his purposes, and to set up the means of existence as the only end of life. The rupture of collaboration between art and prudence is the very drama of our times. It brings

---

[26] *ST*, II-II, q. 50 in its entirety.
[27] *ST*, I-II, q. 57, art. 3, ad 2.

with it the divinization of man who passes himself off as the final end of the universe, and, according to the famous expression of Marx, erects "human self-consciousness as the highest divinity."[28]

[28] Doctoral dissertation, 1841. [Tr.]

VII

DISAPPEARANCE OF THE NATURAL AND THE SUPERNATURAL

THE PROFOUND DIFFER-ences between technology and prudence must not obscure the relations that each continually develops within the everyday life of man.

Let us recall that the intellect of the worker assures man of his *livelihood*, while the practical intellect, prudence, and the moral virtues give him access to *a good life*, and that, crowning the natural aspiration to go from survival to *a good life*, the theoretical intellect[1] and wisdom give him access to what is beyond the human — to *the life of the spirit* that is absorbed in the contemplation of intelligible reality and its Principle. Adding to this movement in which human nature ascends to its perfection, Grace makes man *divinae consors naturae*, sharing in the divine nature, enabling him, if he is completely faithful, to arrive at objective Beatitude, which he would never be able to attain through his own power.

[1] The speculative intellect. [Tr.]

It is clear that, in the state of the present life, *surviving* and *living well*, which prolongs life, constitute the major preoccupation of every person. It is not less obvious that the concern *to survive* and that of *living well* give each other mutual support. Among those who are the most deprived, they go hand-in-hand. Robinson in his obsession to survive ends up meeting Friday. From their rudimentary social relations is born their desire to lead a better life.[2] No man, no matter how close he may be to an animal, is happy with just taking care of his physical needs. If one can in truth state *primum vivere deinde philosophare*,[3] man has no less of a need to live a truly human life in order to sustain his animal life. In him the genus is not disassociated from the species nor the species from the genus. It is not then surprising that art is grafted onto prudence and the moral virtues, nor that these latter are sustained with the help of institutions and various social means which reinforce them. The means which the hardworking rational animal invents in order to compensate for his innate physical indigence have need of the virtues of the practical intellect to be transmitted and these virtues in turn require those means in order to be passed on from one generation to the next.

Now, as St. Thomas tells us, "among the things which man can put to his use, the most important are

---

[2] *Robinson Crusoe* (1719), famed novel of British novelist, journalist, and spy Daniel Defoe (1660–1731). [Tr.]

[3] "First live, then philosophize," attributed to Thomas Hobbes but thought to originate in antiquity. [Tr.]

other men, since man is by nature a social animal."[4] Technical methods in the social realm are themselves at the service of the common good, exactly like those used to transform matter, invented by man and ensuring the use of his most personal good: his life, his uncompromisingly personal existence. The end of the whole always prevails over that of the part, and the end of the whole is the perfection of the part in what is most apparent in it, intellect and will. Through a sort of instinct of the intellect, man, in pursuing the common good, seeks to shore up this perfection, and the social structures he develops, the constitutions he formulates, the political "machine" he creates in order to reinforce his desire to live better are at the service of the common good for which he tirelessly strives as a function of his deepest desire. He becomes a *builder of political communities*, with everything this expression connotes of intertwined art and prudence, to fulfill his desire to live well while seeking the common good.

This is so because man is *naturally* a social animal, as willed by his nature and the Author of that nature. There exists in man a *pre-established order*, to which his intellect, will, and passions are subject so that he can live up to his concept of a man. Aristotle has said it: an isolated individual is either a beast or a god; he is no longer a human being.[5] The need to live in society is so compelling that man has to join forces with others in order to destroy the society which is thwarting him. "The individual against the authorities," to use

4 *Summa Contra Gentiles*, III, 128.
5 *Politics*, I, 1253a. [Tr.]

the expression of Alain,[6] always becomes part of a group, a sect, a party. Yet this activity is anti-nature, and its *antiphysis*[7] can only be carried out with the aid of artificial means. Art, instead of complementing nature in order to support its orientation towards the common good, substitutes for nature here, and as all techniques are at the service of the life of the individual, only contributing to the common good *if the common good still exists*, the result is that the new "society" in place is not a true society but a *dis-society*, the unity of whose members, side by side with each other, can no longer be maintained except by *intensified contrivance*, by the creation out of nothing of a state termed modern. This is the ultimate strategy which makes use of all other strategies to live and survive. The *"grip of steel"* of this State, never before seen in history, more or less tight according to the regime, time, place, circumstances, brings together all the dispersed elements, with the result that, as all contemporary dis-societies are increasingly heading towards their ultimate goal, *we find ourselves in the presence of a totalitarian machinery, artificially constructed and maintained through a thousand coercive techniques* that supplant the natural life of a society and which, no longer the *instrument* of the common good like the traditional State, *is itself its own end*. The individual who stands up against the pre-established social order in which he refuses to serve the common

[6] Emile-Auguste Chartier (1868–1951), called Alain, French philosopher and journalist. From *Le citoyen contre les pouvoirs*, 1926. [Tr.]
[7] What is against nature. [Tr.]

good, demanding his own autonomy, has no other recourse than to use tactics of subterfuge to build an imaginary "society," opposed to nature, which exists only in his imagination and which, in order to materialize, requires that he join together with other similarly uprooted individuals to form a party claiming to be the only one to possess a plan for a humane state. Consequently, this party inexorably aims to establish itself *as the only party*, which *through the ultimate strategy of triumphant physical force* will impose a structure on the amorphous mass of individuals bereft of one.

We are confronted with the most radical Subversion there could be, a subversiveness that rebels against the fundamental principles of the human intellect and will, the principles of identity and finality,[8] and which attributes to the part the function of the whole. The revolt of the individual against his condition of being an individual at the service of all the groups to which he belongs implies, then, the elimination of political prudence, which of all the types of prudence has the greatest role in ordering actions, and is directed towards the highest good in which man can participate here below: the common good, the object of justice in general, i.e., legal justice. This subversiveness necessarily implies the substitution of art for prudence. A world where the "I" is the measure of all things, under the form of the individual "I" or aggrandized through its projection onto the

---

[8] According to the principle of identity, each thing is identical to itself. The principle of finality states that all beings act with an end in view, a specific goal. [Tr.]

collectivity, is a world where technology definitively reigns: *Finis cujuslibet facientis in quantum est faciens, est ipsemet.*[9] When the individual reverses the *natural* order which leads him to serve the common good, *he only has at his disposition the products of his ability to create makeshift substitutes.* For the man deprived of natural means of locomotion, strengthened through the *habitus* of walking, there remain only wooden legs. To get from oneself to another form of oneself, the "I" must multiply the number of crutches. In this exponential collection of prosthetic devices, we have the current Moloch State, the revenge of an offended nature. In the degree to which individuals free themselves from the supposed constraints of society and the common good, through a process of exudation they *produce* the Leviathan that shapes them in the cogs of its ruthless machinery. The suppression of all alienation ends up in the abyss of the ultimate Alienation of man in the new pseudo society, irrevocably imprisoned by his technical intellect.

The question then arises: how has art been able to replace prudence?

We have not a moment's hesitation in answering: *under the influence of a secularized Christianity.*

This is actually not the first time in the history of humanity that individualism has eroded and destroyed societies laboriously built up by nature and human art, and which political prudence, set on a straight course by concern for the common good and justice,

---

[9] The ultimate end of any maker, inasmuch as he is a maker, is himself. *Summa Contra Gentiles*, III, 17. [Tr.]

had maintained in existence. The Greek city-states and the Roman Empire are examples. History is a mass graveyard of vanished societies. For that to happen, a weakening of political prudence suffices. It is the loftiest and most human of all the virtues, the one which COMMANDS and ORDERS the means of effecting man's access to the loftiest and highest of all goods: harmony, unity, the complementary hierarchy of the members of the society of which he is a part. *These means are actions.* We really mean *actions, operations of the intellect and will of the one who exercises authority in the society.* There is no society without a united effort to achieve the common good of each person according to the place he occupies in the community. There are no ordinances regarding these acts without political prudence. There is no political prudence without a mandate. There is no mandate without authority. As soon as authority weakens, social ties deteriorate, degenerate, and break off. "Untune that string," observes Shakespeare, "and hark what discord follows!"[10]

The social bond is an entity having to do with relationship, an entity of the most tenuous: *ens relationis tenuissimum.* It lacks the solidness of a substance. It is composed of the greatest variety of acts, from the most humble and ordinary — small favors, courtesy, even self-serving mutual assistance: "If your neighbor dies, his burden falls on you."[11] — to the most

[10] *Troilus and Cressida.* [Tr.]
[11] *"Le Cheval et l'Âne,"* fable of Jean de la Fontaine (1621–1695), French poet primarily known for his fables.

exceptional and sublime, such as the hero's total gift
of his life as he defends his country. As society is an
entity made up of relationships and the individual is
a substance, even the foremost substance (!), he always
has the tendency to tear apart the weave of this fragile,
but essential, fabric. This is why laws are necessary,
along with the authority to enforce them. The rebel-
lion of the individual against authority, no matter
what form it may take, is common to all times. Nothing is easier than this noncompliance. It is enough
to say "*Me*." It is enough to proclaim, through all
the loudspeakers of our times, *the supremacy of the
human person*. Then disaster falls: the part usurps the
place of the whole, and society, rent asunder, must
continually be artificially socialized.

Without a doubt, Christianity is the only religion
that has emphasized the concept of the person, not
only in the doctrine of the Holy Trinity, where it is
the essential element, but also in the social organization of the Church, charged with preserving and
spreading its message. The Church is the only organization known in history made up of persons. It is
neither national nor international. No social attribute
is required of anyone who is a part of it. One enters it
through baptism alone and the Church baptizes only
individuals, not communities. Divine grace is strictly
personal: *proprias oves vocat nominatim*, God calls
each of His sheep by their name [John 10:3]. It is not
man as belonging to a certain society who is the recip-
ient of grace, but only the individual endowed with
intellect and will. The New Testament substitutes the

concept of the chosen person for the chosen people of the Old Testament. In short, it is the person who receives grace and all the *supernatural* riches it brings with it, who participates in the supernatural society of the Persons of the Holy Trinity and the personal life of Christ, who enables him to know the Father and sends him the Spirit. "Sanctifying grace," writes St. Thomas, "ordains man directly to a union with his ultimate end" with no intermediary.[12] The New Law has the virtue of being the immediate cause of our being brought nearer to our last end.[13] The love which God bears for man is a person-to-person relationship. The Church is a supernatural community of persons in whom God dwells through baptismal grace. It is, in the admirable expression of Bossuet, "Jesus Christ spread abroad and communicated."[14]

Nature cannot arrive at understanding the communion of the person, by definition incommunicable, with other persons, also fundamentally incommunicable, which is accomplished by the supernatural presence of God in each person. "Without Me you can do nothing" [John 15:5]. God, who is immediately and truly present in the individual soul through the gift of grace, more intimate to myself than I am, *intimior intimo meo*, joins the soul to other souls who in turn participate in the deepest Trinitarian intimacy, so that

---

[12] *ST*, I-II, q. 111, art. 5, c.
[13] *ST*, I-II, q. 106, art. 4, c.
[14] Jacques-Bénigne Bossuet (1627–1704), French bishop, theologian, and orator. The citation is from *Pensées chrétiennes et morales* (1704).

each person, contemplating the same supernatural reality (*id*), finds himself, by means of this supernatural reality (*quo*), in communion with what is most profound and incommunicable in the person of his neighbor. To love one's neighbor *in a supernatural way* one must obviously love God supernaturally.

In the very purity of her essence, the Church is the only possible society of persons because it is a *supernatural society* whose *supernatural* common good is God Himself in His intimate depths, revealed to her members in the most intimate part of their being. What is termed Christian personalism only has any *real* meaning at the *supernatural* level, at the level of *what is beyond the human*. If it falls from this level to become "natural," "human," "too human," it is no longer anything but a construct of the imagination, a utopia, destructive of what is human like all the utopias which man incarnates in his behavior, the prodigious destructive power of which we shall proceed to analyze.

We note as a preliminary that according to the old saying grace does not destroy nature, rather it elevates it to a level it never would have been able to attain on its own and *it presupposes nature*. It is quite evident that there is no supernatural if there is no *natural*, if there is no human *nature*, if there is no animal *naturally* political.[15] If natural happiness, that is, the possession and enjoyment of the common good, is impossible without the integration of the

---

[15] As we have seen, the use of "political" has the connotation of "social." [Tr.]

individual into a political community, without prudence and a political authority that determine and
put into operation the means adapted to this final
end in the temporal order, supernatural beatitude
presupposes subordination of the person to the whole
of which he is a part. We do not arrive at the supernatural end without the strictly required intermediary
of the natural end. Without a social order, without
political prudence, Christ cannot be spread abroad
and communicated. It would be a perpetual miracle
if God were to produce in each person in and of
himself the conditions for attaining the supernatural
order: a certain knowledge, a certain good will, the
elementary practice of the cardinal virtues which
make of the individual a human being and which can
only be acquired in a society. It would be necessary
that in speaking to each person *nominatim*,[16] God
were to create in him all these elements constitutive
of man. God would necessarily create each man out
of nothingness. Which is an absurdity.

In fact, God calls the person *nominatim* because
each person, far from being the *end* of society, is
the *effect* of the social order established by political
prudence. If the person is, according to the definition
of Boethius, "an individual substance of a rational
nature,"[17] he only attains to a degree of intellectual
perfection if he benefits from the social order to

[16] By name. [Tr.]
[17] Roman Christian polymath (c. 480–524) whose philosophical
work was influential in the Middle Ages and beyond. The citation
is from *Contra Eutychen*. [Tr.]

which his activities are subordinated. Supposing such a thing were possible, an individual with a rational nature who would hypothetically be isolated from any relationship with others, and consequently from any elementary form of society, would never enjoy the gift of speech. He would understand nothing. How then, deaf and mute, would he be able to receive and spread abroad the Word of God? It is shameful to have to bring these truisms to mind. Nothing can compensate for the political nature of man. The mark of the social is branded onto his inmost being. Without it, grace does not penetrate. God the Redeemer does not deny God the Creator.

Two consequences immediately follow of fundamental importance in an age where secularism pervades thinking.

The first is that where the temporal common good is not supported, even superficially, by the political prudence of the leader, the evangelical message is paralyzed. For grace to be poured out, a minimum *natural* social order is required, based on the moral virtues, legal justice which requires that each person serve the common good according to the place he occupies in society, distributive justice which makes a return to each person according to the services he has rendered, commutative justice which governs private transactions, and also political prudence, which identifies the means suited to maintaining unity and peace among members of society. It was not in times of civil wars tearing apart the republic that Christ was born, but when the empire extended over the whole world the protective mantle of the *pax romana*. An age like ours, when class conflict rages, political parties clash with each other, pressure groups live off the common good and devour it, revolution is always brewing, the great imperial blocs are in conflict, nations are at each other's throats, innocent peoples are the targets of the most shameful extortion, hold ups[18] and hostage taking all become international institutions more powerful than the "Whatever you may call it,"[19] such an age corresponds to that of the decline of Christianity. Divisive democracy is the mortal enemy of supernatural faith, hope, and charity. It neutralizes and annihilates the possibilities for them to be practiced, and causes their respective *habitus* to atrophy. But it is unfortunately only too true that we see only what we want to. The blindness of today's clergy is in this respect incurable: *aggiornamento* in a world dying of democracy has gouged out their eyes.

The second consequence is just as important: where there is no more *natural* religion, where God does not receive the worship which is due Him, where the virtue of religion, part of the virtue of justice is no longer practiced; where society is becoming secularized; where the common good of the group does not rely on the transcendent, unchanging Common Good, the final end of human life; and where the contingencies of existence can no longer be effectively

---

[18] In English in original. [Tr.]
[19] *Machin* in French, a term used to identify something the name of which one cannot quite remember, possibly referring here to Christianity. [Tr.]

regulated by political prudence because their various possibilities are no longer evaluated with the help of a constant criterion, the seed of grace falls on rocky ground. Political prudence *necessarily* requires support from religion to be exercised because temporal justice, guardian of the common good, can only prevent changes in mores, always detrimental to the stability of the common good, if the mores themselves bank their stability on their relationship to a Being who is unchanging. Modern societies, organized according to "neutral" principles and the separation of Church and state, rapidly see the concept of their common good erased from the minds of citizens. But the "alliance between Throne and Altar" is not only indispensable to the Throne, but also to the Altar itself, in the great degree to which, as we have said, the *natural* common good constitutes the terrain supportive of the practice of the virtues whose own end is the *supernatural* common good. A state which does not make people virtuous according to the ways of nature corresponds to a Church where the theological virtues yield to revolutionary policies and a Christianity radically devoid of any supernatural meaning. The secularized state ultimately becomes transformed into an atheistic state, which converges with an atheistic Church, an atheistic hierarchy, an atheistic Inquisition, the last stage of the denial of both the temporal and the spiritual common good, when political prudence is eliminated to the advantage of a merciless police apparatus, when the communion of saints gives way to communism, to utopian collective ownership in which the new ruling class, a *new atheistic clergy*, takes charge as the only beneficiary, to the inalienable possession of goods,[20] nominally possessed by all but actually possessed by few.

How can grace sprout up through such a block of reinforced concrete? There is no utopia more *outrageous* than the senseless project of "baptizing" atheist communism, the result of the simultaneous loss of the virtue of *moderation*, prudence, and the sense of the *supernatural*.

Therein lies the whole tragedy of the modern world: in *the disappearance of both the natural and the supernatural,* from the temporal common good, the means to which are determined by political prudence, and also from the spiritual common good, brought about through grace, ending in *the curse of constructs or artificial "systems" meant to provide a framework somehow for individuals no longer bound together through a common natural or supernatural end*. We do not have to mull over it for a long time to discover the cause, the sole cause of the mortal illness affecting contemporary societies: *It is the immersion of a corrupted Christianity into what is time-bound.* "If salt loses its savor, how can it be made salty again?" [Matt. 5:13]. Christianity has given birth to the only society of persons that is not a square circle and which can only exist at the supernatural level. A society is not made up of individuals, but of animals who are

---

[20] *Biens de mainmorte*, referring to the possession of lands or other goods endowed to a religious or other organization in perpetuity. [Tr.]

naturally political, already united among themselves by the desire to live and by the aspiration to live well, and whose desires are channeled into institutions by prudence and art. *Society comes before the person, who in reality can only be the effect of it.* If Christianity has succeeded in building a society of persons, it is because those persons have received the grace of sharing in the divine life which *supernaturally* establishes their mutual relationship. In this sense, the Church is the only society which is subsequent to the person. There is no other. There cannot be another. It alone is ordered to the SUPERNATURAL salvation of the person who possesses grace.

But if the supernatural yeast goes bad, if societies that have set up a modus vivendi between the natural and supernatural witness the rupture of this alliance, the mark of the latter on the former persists. Societies that were Christian do not cast off the supernatural like a worn-out, outmoded garment which must be replaced with a more "modern" one. Christianity is as were it their very skin through which they breathe. It is enough to appeal to history to observe to what degree Christianity was as one with them, forming one living body. When their skin is ripped off, these societies produce another, purulent, gangrenous, with an infection against which their relative natural and supernatural immunization no longer works, an infection which reaches essential organs and destroys organic relations among them. This dreadful illness is individualism, personalism. As soon as the substance of the supernatural order vanishes, the form remains and projects itself onto the temporal, penetrating it and engendering that uninhabitable monster, modern "society," made up of individuals free from any obligation to the common good, the natural law, or the eternal law, perfectly autonomous, strictly incapable of communicating among themselves (since the person in and of himself is incommunicable save in the supernatural order) and fundamentally incapable of constructing a society together.

This "society" supposedly devoted to the "promotion" of the human person is in reality, let us never tire of saying this, a *dis-society the sole bond of which can only be a counterfeit of supernatural grace: the religion of humanity, a camouflage for the cult of adoration which the human person renders to himself.* The human person whose supernatural end is God, and an intimate relationship with Him, can only worship himself once his relation to the Transcendent is pushed back to the temporal. There is no other end except God or Me. Christianity transposed to the temporal and transformed into a political ideology has gotten rid of God so that the "I" can act on its own account. The one and only name of this appalling subversion is: *modern democracy*, a system which, as its creator, Rousseau, avowed, is only suitable for a people of gods.[21] Liberal democracies such as communist democracies and democracies called Christian are the products of a project to replace Christianity, where imitations of the theological virtues become

[21] *The Social Contract* (1762). [Tr.]

"anthropological." According to Chesterton's brilliant formula, which must be continually cited since it goes to the heart of the modern drama, "Take away the supernatural, and what remains is the unnatural,"[22] i.e., the ARTIFICIAL. We live, we make a pretense of living, starting from the dissolution of medieval Christianity, in a *factitious* social setting, in a "*society*" which no longer owes anything to the social nature of man or to the supernatural, a source of consolation to him, and which radically aims to be the work of man, the creation of the *homo faber*.

Contemporary "society" was foreshadowed in the society which the Renaissance and the Reformation gave birth to. The dazzling explosion of *artifices*[23] of every kind which bursts forth at the Renaissance must not make us forget that that was the time when the most frenzied individualism detonated *following the breakdown of medieval Christianity and the supernatural which it conveyed to souls*. Certainly the natural bases of life in society were hardly undermined: the natural at that stage had not yet developed into the artificial, and the bastions of social resistance were still powerful, widespread, numerous, especially in the country which at that time comprehended most of Europe, though they had next to no real political influence. Yet all the elites in power were affected, even at the highest reaches of the Church. *A profound reform in the concept of truth was effected.*

[22] *Heretics* (1905). [Tr.]
[23] *Feu d'artifices*, fireworks with a double entendre in this play on words. [Tr.]

Eugenio Garin writes, "After human thought endeavored for many centuries to develop a philosophy of religious hope — a sign under which all things were viewed — man's intellect directed all its efforts *towards man as a poet, his polity, that worldly nature* which was being conquered."[24] In Aristotelian and Thomist terms, *the intellect of the artisan, maker of artificial things, substitutes for the practical intellect directed to its end by the appetite for the natural and supernatural Sovereign Good.* As has been said a thousand times, *an anthropocentric concept of the world is substituted for a theocentric concept.* St. Thomas indicates the course of this reversal of perspective with unequaled lucidity. Once again we cite his precise diagnostic, luminous, congruent with reality: *Finis facientis inquantum est facientis est* IPSEMET.

For Bacon, to know is to modify the data of experience; it is *to make, to transform, what is real*: knowing goes hand in hand with knowing how, technique, and art. With the numerous inventors, astrologers, magicians, and scientists of that age, the dominant idea was the plasticity of things, their obedience to the dominating, transforming will of man. As Eugenio Garin further writes, contrary to Aristotle and St. Thomas "the humanists insisted on the freedom *to create*, on the man *who constructs objects and constructs himself*, who does not copy from a model but designs it, who like God is a *creator, a "poet,"* with the ever-recurring risk of a failure *which calls reality*

[24] *Moyen-Age et Renaissance*, Paris, 1969, p. 9.

into question."[25] A new current of thought emerges where truth is no longer thought corresponding to reality, but the opposite, reality corresponding to thought, which impresses itself onto the form of reality. The poetic intellect succeeds the contemplative intellect: "Sculpt and chisel yourself according to the form you desire; change the world according to the decisions of your mind and the aspirations of your will." We recognize the famous words of Telesio[26] on the men of his age who "were rivals of God and fought with him . . . as if they themselves had made the world."[27] It is then, when they have turned their backs on the Aristotelian and Thomist conception of the world that the techniques of alchemy and magic arise which aim to change things, along with experimental techniques that strive to use the laws of nature in order to make the world docile to the exigencies of those who make use of them.

Human activity *is no longer governed by prudence but by art*, method, technique, know-how, skill, dexterity, by a thousand and one formulas thanks to which a person makes himself valued, surpasses others, triumphs over his adversary, submits the world to his will and power. Prudence disappears, as it is its objectivity that dies. It is no longer a matter of being obedient to the ends of the moral virtues while finding the means to attain these ends, but rather of submitting others, and the world, to one's desires,

[25] Ibid., p. 28.
[26] Italian philosopher and scientist (1509–1588). [Tr.]
[27] Cited by Eugenio Garin, p. 81.

to one's triumphant subjectivity, thanks to proven means and infallible techniques. The notion of the common good and political prudence disappears to the benefit of the good of the individual alone and his astuteness. Machiavelli is not the tutor of the Christian Prince, nor, no matter what has been said of this, of the pagan Prince, but of the Tamer of the "great beast," the people, with whose powerful backing he establishes his personal seat of power. Politics becomes, as Voltaire put it, "the art of deliberately lying,"[28] no longer the politics of making people virtuous, as St. Thomas, following Aristotle, imagined in his candor. Craftiness, the use of "means which are not correct, but deceptive and counterfeit,"[29] and guile, "which executes them," particularly "through the use of words,"[30] are, as St. Thomas teaches, *vices opposed to prudence in their deceptive similarity to it*. Art, the twin brother of prudence, has now completely replaced it.

As a consequence, "society," or more precisely "dis-society," is no longer considered in its natural end and organic structure as ordered to the common good, unity, and peace among citizens. It is a soft clay into which penetrates, through ruse or violence or both, *the reasoning of the strongest*, of the most cynical. From the Age of the Renaissance to our times, when propaganda bombards minds, obliterates their ability to react, prevents their access to what is true through

[28] *Le siècle de Louis XIV* (1751). [Tr.]
[29] *ST*, II-II, q. 55, art. 3, c..
[30] *ST*, II-II, q. 55, art. 4, c. and ad 2.

disinformation, and agglomerates them into a mold, continuity has been interrupted. The only difference is that today the will to power is deployed with the complicity, if not enthusiasm, of the hoodwinked victims, persuaded that their leaders are their servants and that the "new society," presented before their astonished eyes as a dazzling mirage, is constructed for the complete fulfillment of their feeble persons.

Such individualism would never have been able to be spread abroad without the weakening of the sense of the supernatural, first in the minds of the elite, then in those of the masses, without the deliberate or tacit repudiation of the ordering of the person to the common good which all de-Christianization entails. The frenzied research on every kind of technology, in all sectors, from the physical world to the government of societies, is caused by a decline in the degree to which Christianity is a vital force in the human heart, with the supernatural end no longer in view; consequently, the natural end, with the subsequent irrelevance of the virtue of prudence, is necessarily replaced by art.

It is hardly necessary to show, following the famous studies of Max Weber, how Protestant individualism is linked to technical progress in all countries where Catholicism was supplanted. *Finis ultimus cujuslibet facientis inquantum est faciens, est ipsemet.* The individual, left alone, bereft of the protecting framework of the Church and Tradition, reduced to being his own pope, left to his own interpretation of Scripture, has no other recourse than to *construct for himself*, out

of his own subjectivity, his own *ipseity*,[31] a new supernatural world. Confronted with this staggering, enor-
mous, never-ending task, where he finds himself alone
with God, whose transcendence overwhelms him, he
is in the throes of an implacable anguish. He is cut
off from the channel through which grace comes to
him: the Church, which is nothing other than "Jesus
Christ spread abroad and communicated" to people.
He finds himself in a state of total insecurity about
his salvation. What is there in the presence of the
Infinite save a nothingness teeming with sins? Good
works and the practice of the moral virtues regulated
by prudence are only a camouflage for the frightful
flight which distances him from God. It is within the
grip of sin that he experiences the mortal absence of
God in his soul. *Pecca fortiter*,[32] sin boldly and you
will feel a greater need of being saved. Salvation can
only come from without, from the inscrutable will of
God, the divine arbiter. *Credo quia absurdum.*[33] It is
by *sola gratia, sola fide*[34] that man can escape eternal
damnation. Nothing at all guarantees the redemption
of man left to himself, of the human person separated
from the Church. Neither the practical intellect nor
prudence, with their modest lights, manages to break
through the dark shadows. The speculative intellect

[31] Selfhood, individual identity. [Tr.]
[32] Martin Luther's words, "sin boldly"; he continues, "but believe
more boldly," an encapsulation of his doctrine that once he is
saved, sin cannot separate the sinner from God. [Tr.]
[33] A misconstrual dating from the Enlightenment of an expression of Tertullian's. [Tr.]
[34] By grace alone, by faith alone. [Tr.]

is still more powerless with its complete finiteness. Reason is "the devil's whore,"[35] the attraction to which irrevocably distances us from God.

As Étienne Gilson insightfully writes, it is matter of nothing less, in this struggle of Protestantism against the Catholic Church, "than knowing if the Christian concept of the supernatural would accept the old idea of the natural to complement it, or would definitively destroy it in order to take its place. That was what was at stake in the Reformation": a supernatural devoid of any relationship to nature, to the speculative intellect of man whose object is radically superhuman, to the practical intellect whose end is infinitely remote, to prudence humanly incapable of finding the means to attain that end, even through a veil, and *which leaves man with only the ability to use his poetic intellect, transforming the world, henceforth an infallible sign of divine election. Technology becomes the annunciation, the promise, the index, the manifestation, the proof of salvation.* In his famous theses of 1517 against scholastic theology,[36] "Luther aimed at the vital organs of the thought of man," reasoning in its twofold function, speculative and practical, and particularly *prudence*, a virtue of the intellect which renders the works of man good.[37] Man is left with only the art of shaping the universe *for his own person*. Once again, *finis ultimus cujuslibet*

[35] An expression used by Luther. See, for example, his sermon of January 17, 1546. [Tr.]
[36] Not to be confused with his 95 theses against indulgences, posted later in 1517. [Tr.]
[37] Étienne Gilson, *Héloïse et Abélard*, Paris, 1938, p. 200.

facientis inquantum est faciens, est IPSEMET. In a world where individualism triumphs, *contemplation and action* give way to *making*.

Making EVERYTHING. For everything is to be remade by the person who becomes the center of the universe, and around whom orbits even the salvific will of God. Everything tends to occur as curated by transformative activity because everything *becomes radicalized* under pressure from a multitude of individuals, each one becoming in some way the end of all things. This is total subversion: it penetrates to the inmost depths of the human being in his relationship with himself, with others, with the world, and with God. As this project is counter to nature, artifice after artifice is required in order to create utopia. Step by step, the substitution of the artificial for the natural penetrates society, the state, and the human being defined as a naturally political animal. It is a matter of nothing less than inverting the subordination of the person to the natural and supernatural common good and, according to the expression of Marx, to set up human self-awareness as a divinity. The *omnia tendunt assimilari Deo*,[38] the universal movement of all things towards God, which at the human level involves the exercise of the virtue of legal justice and conformity to political prudence according to St. Thomas, yields to *omnia tendunt assimilari homini*.[39] Everything in the world must bear the mark

[38] All things tend to be like God. *Summa Contra Gentiles*, III, 19. [Tr.]
[39] All things tend to be like man. [Tr.]

of man, everything must be transformed by him and for his sake. This is the revolutionary phenomenon which is still wreaking havoc.

From the Renaissance and the Reformation to the political Revolution, there is no path of continuity. From the Renaissance and the Reformation to the industrial revolution, there is only an uninterrupted accumulation of technical methods that endlessly evolve because people attempt the *impossible, daunting task* of artificially constructing a "society" of which they personally will be the end. This unattainable project only ends in a plethora of means. A civilization of *making*, a "society" based solely on economics, is the utopia to end all utopias. Political revolution and the industrial revolution could only succeed if it was possible to construct a society of persons. The project, from its inception, was doomed to fail. The only society of persons that could exist is *supernatural*: it is the Church, the Kingdom of God where the common good, the Holy Trinity of Persons, will only be fully realized after the end of the world, when there will be a *new earth* and a *new heaven*, according to the prediction of the *Apocalypse* [Rev. 21:1]. The degeneration of Christianity into what is time-bound, the determination to build a new earthly paradise here below, where the human person would be the beginning and the end, is the one and only cause of the political revolution and the economic revolution which are destabilizing the contemporary world. The denial of the objective supernatural and the consequent contempt for the

natural are at the origins of the invasion of technology — and finally of the state, the omnipotent tool
of technology — into the domains of Wisdom and
Prudence that it displaces and exterminates.

This is why there are no more wise persons, only
experts, no more prudent persons, only the adept and
wily, and the vast crowds of those who are duped.
This is why the senseless scheme of building a "new
society" and a "new man" thanks to the conjoined
strategies of the applied sciences and politics — or,
more precisely, what politics has become — is being
continued in the chimerical religion of Man and
the Future. Marx once again had the diabolically
apt expression for it: man is the future of man. So
thought the young Renan, who had recently trans-
ferred the divine attribution of the Second Person
of the Trinity to the Humanity to come when he
predicted the advent of the *Religion of the Future*.[40]
However it was to the inspired Ballanche, the pre-
cursor of all today's gadabout[41] clergy, that we owe
the precise diagnosis for the current situation: "The
Christian genius has become the social genius."[42]
Becoming limited to living in the dimension of time,
and secularized, the society of persons established
by the supernatural message of Christ has been

[40] Ernest Renan (1823–1892), French philosopher and historian
of religion, who held science to be the religion of the future. See
L'Avenir de la science, 1890. [Tr.]
[41] *Gyrovagues*, gyrovagues, independent itinerant monks who
relied on charity to survive. [Tr.]
[42] *Oeuvres* complètes, vol. III, Paris, 1833, p. 19. [Pierre-Simon
Ballanche (1776–1847), French philosopher. (Tr.)]

transformed into a factor of the dissolution of all
natural societies to the benefit of the human person,
henceforth compelled to build a new "society" from
the ground up which will have a corrupt, secularized
Christianity as its religion. For the celebration of
the centenary of the revolution in 1889, a member
of the Comédie Française[43] would sing the final
line of a hymn to Reason as the architect of the
new world, "Man who has become a god through
me!" The revolution is from then on a "miniature
of the last judgment"—the "age of Christianity in
spirit and truth begins with the abolition of the rule
of priests."[44] The *poetic* genius replaces grace. The
writer exercises his priesthood. The craftsman first
of all and then the technician and those who follow
in their wake are going to transfigure the world and
create the Kingdom of God on earth.

The age of the creative *intelligentia* is dawning.
The new theocracy—or "anthropocracy"—is being
established on Patmos,[45] in the forum, the press, in
front of the microphone, in all the media, with the
support of experts, psychologists, sociologists, philosophers, economists, engineers of the material and
the spiritual, and is *trying, with all available means*,
using strategies in turn coarse or refined, blunt or

[43] Founded in 1680, one of the few state theaters in France. [Tr.]
[44] Louis-Claude de Saint-Martin, *Mon portrait historique et
philosophique*, Paris, 1961, no. 707. [Originally published in partial
form in 1807. Saint-Martin (1743–1803) was a French philosopher.
[Tr.]]
[45] Island where St. John, in exile, wrote the book of Revelation.
[Tr.]

subtle, to found *a new Christianity*[46] WITHOUT THE SUPERNATURAL, a purely human Christianity where man is the end of man: IPSEMET.[47]

The Catholic Church and the majority of Christian churches had up to now guarded against these forms of lunacy. But suddenly the dike was breached. With unparalleled *imprudence*, the good Pope John XXIII uttered the fatal word: *aggiornamento*. The modern world, the result of the "naturalization of Christianity,"[48] or, more accurately, of a Christianity amputated from its supernatural objective, and, as a result, incapable of perfecting nature and fit only to destroy it, has invaded the Church and its hierarchy, *who have enlisted in its service*. They have thus become the *instruments* of its increasing falsification and of the concomitant reversal of the end to be attained from God into man, and also of their own self-destruction. The Church, a *supernatural society of persons*, in renouncing her essential vocation, thus becomes the most effective *means* at the disposal of Subversion in order to convert the impossible "personalist" democracy into totalitarian socialism. The Church, now part of the system, is slowly, inexorably becoming effaced before it. As Cardinal Liénart,[49] responsible, along with many

---

[46] As is known, this is the title of a little work by Saint-Simon. [Henri de Saint-Simon (1760–1825), French political and economic theorist, not to be confused with his relative Louis de Rouvroy, Duke of Saint-Simon, whose memoirs are a classic of French literature. [Tr.]]

[47] He himself. [Tr.]

[48] Pierre-Maurice Masson, *La religion de Jean-Jacques Rousseau*, vol. I, Paris, 1916, p. 279.

[49] Achille Liénart (1884–1973), Bishop of Lille. [Tr.]

others, for this transformation, confided to Canon Vancourt,[50] who made it public, "Humanly speaking, the Church can no longer be saved." Her caricature is devouring her.

With the Church (temporarily at least for the believer, who knows that she has received the promise of eternal life) our most certain basis for the hope that humanity will return to social health has disappeared or is dangerously weakened.

[50] Raymond Vancourt, professor at the University of Lille. [Tr.]

VIII
CONCLUSION

THE HORIZON IS DARK AND the days to come are only promising for the optimist who is walking at the edge of the abyss with the blind security of a sleepwalker. We need nothing less than robust virtue, natural and supernatural, not to abandon the fight which we are witnessing against the total reversal of all ultimate goals.

Our conclusion will necessarily be brief and our prognosis summary. Unless one were a pseudo-mystic who claims to be a seer and prophet, one could not possibly pierce through the turbulent clouds that are amassing before our eyes.

Nevertheless two essential points stand out sharply to the prudent man, warned by past experience and endowed with basic good sense.

There is no morality, personal or social, without a stable standard or one considered as such. Aristotle and St. Thomas in this connection put their trust in the law, in the "consideration of various forms of government,"[1] *quales politiae salvant civitates*,[2] and,

---

[1] *Nic. Eth.*, X, 9, 1181 and *CNE*, 2180.
[2] Which of the various forms of government preserve states, *CNE*, 2180. [Tr.]

ultimately in the natural law, reflection of the eternal law according to the Angelic Doctor. Today the *artificial* has virtually eliminated all traces of the *natural* from politics, and with it all concern for the temporal common good. The possibilities for a return *to the nature of things* prove to be strikingly reduced.

The only thing emerging from the night is a faint *supernatural* light, still spreading Christianity abroad in souls, but whose influence on those in charge of the government of the Church, *won over by the artificialized*, is virtually nil. Nevertheless it is from the supernatural, from the energetic, unfailing, unflinching preservation of its presence, that the natural will be reborn. The clergy, from the bottom to the top of the hierarchy, have forgotten this. They are exclusively concerned about the temporal. "The will of God is keeping busy," said an empty-headed bishop who no longer knows that "the will of God is our sanctification": *haec est voluntas Dei, sanctificatio vestra* [I Thess. 4:3]. But there is no supernatural without the presence of the natural: *gratia naturam supponit.*[3] Where we find the supernatural, the natural is present.

It is easy to draw a conclusion from this. History confirms it. It is neither warriors nor diplomats who have made Western civilization into whatever it has of the human, it is SAINTS. When the hierarchy devote themselves to their sanctification and the supernatural love of God, our world, undermined by what is sham

---

[3] Grace builds on nature. [Tr.]

and subjective in individuals and the collectivity, will recover its equilibrium: the temporal common good will provide a goal for activities *in a consistent manner and political prudence* will reveal the means, because the supernatural and *unchangeable* Common Good will yet manifest its actual presence in the world.

There remains the great problem of industrial civilization extended to the four corners of the world through the eviction of prudence by technology and the universalization of a Christianity devoid of its supernatural substance. Its prodigious dynamism has exorcised the specter of penury from three-quarters of the globe. But at what price? At the price of the sacrifice of all objectives other than that of means multiplied abundantly. At the price of an internal contradiction that will infallibly bring about its death if the remedy is not supplied in time to address the following: the pursuit of *means* that have become the *end* of human life, the decline and disappearance of natural communities, the pursuit of productivity for the sake of productivity, the exhaustion of the powers of nature, the absorption of the private domain into the public domain, and finally the substitution of *living*, considered as the only attribute of man, for *living well*, to which man living in society has always aspired. In the optics of this civilization — if one can still call it that — man is made in order to produce and consume. To produce in order to consume and to consume in order to produce is henceforth the only law that rules humanity. The worker is the only human being worthy of the name.

But everything has a price: *finis cujuslibet facientis in quantum facientis est* IPSEMET. The objective of the man who transforms matter can only be himself, considered individually or collectively. Humanity will soon be nothing more than a fantastical factory where people will produce at its entrance and consume at its exit, in an endless cycle whose infallible rhythm will be assured by the omnipotent state, its Merovingian power actually residing in the mayors of the palace.[4] For Marx and his contemporary ecclesiastical recruits, this would be the reopening of the Garden of Eden. But hell, as Simone Weil said, is mistakenly believing one is in paradise.[5] Never have people been so stupid, now that they have technology at their disposal, which allows them to *live* without being fixed almost exclusively on the anxiety of providing for their subsistence, as were their ancestors in the past. They have lost the very simple secret of *living well* without which "the economy of affluence," in which they get bogged down, continually generates new insoluble problems. The dynamism of the modern economy which, however, ensures the means to *live* for the great majority of people in today's industrialized societies, has become a kind of endemic fever, rarely remittent, often paroxysmal, always getting worse. This is the sign of a

[4] The Merovingian kings ruled the Franks from the mid-fifth century until 751. In the last century of their reign, power was increasingly in the hands of a powerful official called the mayor of the palace. [Tr.]
[5] *La pesanteur et la grâce* (1947). Simone Weil (1909–1943) was a French philosopher and political activist. Attracted to Catholicism, she was never baptized. [Tr.]

pathological state. Health, no matter what Dr. Knock may say about it,[6] is the natural state of man. The "miracles of technology" are being changed into lies because there is no politics worthy of the name and especially because there is no longer an economic policy.

The reason for this is clear. Due to the ultimate objective of the state and the *ipsemet* which characterizes it, the economy and technology that drive it belong ENTIRELY *to the private sector*. It is doubtlessly no longer geared to the individual as in the historical age of the harvest and the hunt. People then very quickly saw that they had to group together to ensure their subsistence and survival. Yet these associations are precarious: they are far from having the lifespan of states and civilizations. They differ fundamentally from these latter in their end. Never do economics and technology *taken as such* ensure the common good, ultimate end of man living in society here below, for which political prudence identifies the means. The public sphere is ENTIRELY political. A political society that is at the same time and in the same respect an economic society, the dream of socialism, is a contradiction in terms. Merely *living* is not and cannot be *living well*. The *bonum utile* cannot be the *bonum honestum*.[7] They are on two different levels.

---

[6] *Knock ou le Triomphe de la médicine* (1923), a satirical play in which Dr. Knock convinces the villagers in his practice that they are not in good health, to his financial advantage. Perhaps the best-known work of the French playwright and novelist Jules Romains (1885–1972). [Tr.]

[7] The useful good contrasted with the virtuous, or moral, good. [Tr.]

In fact, though under the influence of a degraded and secularized Christianity, the individual has first slowly, then turbulently, set himself up as the final end of the social order. The activity of the hardworking intellect who proceeds from "me" to "me" is transposed to the sphere of the common good which he has demolished. Man works in order to live and life (like death) is what is most personal to him. The whole has then become the means by which the part aspires to set itself up as the whole. This failed project is always taken up anew with the help of ever more powerful technology, doomed in turn to failure.

This vicious circle, where the distinctions between the private and public spheres are blurred, must be broken. Economics must be separated from politics, so that each may be restored to its own nature and purpose. One cannot go against the nature of things without one's endeavor ending in catastrophe.

That does not mean that economics is an autonomous sector, radically foreign to politics. It is, however, subordinated to politics so closely that constant relations between them are formed and the most important machinery of the state, in our *current* situation, is the *political economy*. This is exactly what has most gone awry in all states. By *political economy* we do not mean the constant intervention of pressure groups in the life of the state, nor, through an inevitable recurrence of things, permanent state intervention in economic life. A reciprocal parasitism, in which the parts devour the whole and the whole the parts, is termed nothing other than a political economy. The state, as a function of its sovereignty, must be the judge among parts, its role entirely that of arbitration in conflicts of interest that flare up. The role of the economy is wholly to serve the consumer in flesh and blood: a collective entity consumes nothing; there must be a physical body, belonging to an individual, in order to consume material goods, and a collectivity has no body. It follows that the only system that addresses the goal of the economy is the *market economy*, in which the producer who best serves the interests of his customers is at every instant "elected" by the market economy and maintains his status as producer. Such a system cannot be left to itself. Subordinated to politics, it must be constantly overseen by politics so that it does not oppose the common good and serves the natural aspirations of man to live well. The ancients did not hesitate to state that the end of the state is to make people virtuous. The function of the state in this regard is to monitor the morality of the economic system with respect to its purpose: service to the consumer. More exactly, the current dynamic economy should have its *charter*,[8] analogous to the corporate charters of the Middle Ages which, in a static economic situation, guaranteed the morality of the market and its purpose.

We do not claim that it would be an easy thing to try in this way to domesticate the savage dynamism of today's technology and economy, to adapt useful

---

[8] The foundational principles of this charter are articulated in *Solution Sociale* by H. de Lovinfosse and G. Thibon, Journées de Waasmunster, 1953, p. 171. Twenty years later, they are still relevant.

products to a moral purpose, to align self-interest with duty, to reconcile the desire to live with that of living better, to attenuate to the extent possible the fallacious antagonism — romantic like everything that involves a bastardized Christianity — between the individual and society. On the contrary, we would even be tempted to say that people of our times, captivated by technology, presumed capable of staving off all their troubles, in the grip of individual, collective, and even altruistic narcissism, would only address this if they were on the verge of a catastrophe, or perhaps not until after one. Setting the economy right, restoring the dis-society to a society, will not be done in a day. But we need not wait in order to undertake what is necessary. It is the business of the philosopher to cast into meaningful words referring to eternal realities what others quite superior to him will carry out by their deeds.

These will be human acts, carried out through the human virtues that will enable them to attain the objective purpose of man, and through the most human among them which provides objective means: perfect prudence, political prudence, and not "subjective human awareness conceived as the highest divinity."